THE
MAGIC UMBRELLA
AND OTHER STORIES
FOR TELLING

THE
MAGIC UMBRELLA
AND OTHER STORIES
FOR TELLING

With notes on how to
tell them by
EILEEN COLWELL
Drawings by
SHIRLEY FELTS

DAVID McKAY COMPANY, INC.
New York

Library of Congress Catalog Card Number: 76-53970
ISBN: 0-679-20400-8

10 9 8 7 6 5 4 3 2 1
Manufactured in the United States of America

Acknowledgments

Every effort has been made to trace the ownership of the copyright material in this book. It is the publishers' belief that the necessary permissions from publishers, authors, and authorised agents have been obtained, but in the event of any question arising as to the use of any material, the publishers, while expressing regret for any error unconsciously made, will be pleased to make the necessary corrections in future editions of this book.

Thanks are due to the following for permission to reprint copyright material: The Society of Authors as the literary representative of the Estate of the late Rose Fyleman for 'The Magic Umbrella' from *Good Morning Tales,* published by Methuen & Co Ltd; Friends' Home Service Committee as the Literary Executor of the late L. V. Hodgkin for 'Fierce Feathers' from *A Book of Quaker Saints*; The Literary Trustees of Walter de la Mare and The Society of Authors as their representative for 'Molly Whuppie' from *Tales Told Again*, published by Faber & Faber Ltd; Oxford University Press for 'The Death of Balder' from *Tales of the Norse Gods and Heroes* by Barbara Leonie Picard; David Higham Associates for 'The Elephant's Picnic' from *Don't Blame Me and Other Stories* by Richard Hughes, published by Chatto & Windus; Penguin Books Ltd for 'The Woman of the Sea' by Helen Waddell from *The Princess Splendour and Other Stories* edited by Eileen Colwell (Longman Young Books 1969) pp. 119–162, Copyright © Longman Group Ltd 1969; David Higham Associates for 'A Girl Calling' from *Silver Sand and Snow* by the late Miss Eleanor Farjeon, published by Michael Joseph; the Executors of the Laurence Housman Estate for 'Rocking-Horse Land' from *Moonshine and Clover*, published by Jonathan Cape Ltd; Penguin Books Ltd and Harper & Row Publishers Inc for 'Zlateh the Goat' from *Zlateh the Goat and Other Stories* by Isaac Bashevis Singer, translated by the author and Elizabeth Shub (Longman Young Books 1970), Text copyright © Isaac Bashevis Singer 1966; Methuen & Co Ltd for 'Annabelle' from *Time and Again Stories* (1970) by Donald Bissett; David Higham Associates for 'Rabbit and the Wolves' from *Tortoise Tales* by Ruth Manning-Sanders, published by Eyre Methuen Ltd; David Higham Associates for 'Nella's Dancing Shoes' from *Italian Peepshow* by the late Miss Eleanor Farjeon, published by Oxford University Press; Ian Serraillier for 'The Summit' from *Everest Climbed* from

Contents

The Magic Umbrella 6ᵀ

There was once a wizard who had a magic umbrella. One night he went to a meeting of wizards and witches in the market place and when it was over he forgot his umbrella and left it leaning against a stall. Next morning an old farmer found it there and, as no one claimed it, he took it home to his wife.

Now *we* know—but the farmer and his wife didn't, of course—that this was a magic umbrella. If you held it open in your hand and counted three, you found yourself at home. If you counted five, you found yourself where you most wanted to be at that moment. If you counted *seven*, there you were floating round

9

and round the top of the nearest church steeple!

When next the farmer's wife went to market, she took the magic umbrella with her because it was raining. As she sat at her stall in the afternoon with the umbrella open in her hand, a boy came up and asked if she had any eggs left. 'Why, yes,' said the old lady, 'just three. Hold out your basket,' and she counted the eggs into it. ONE-TWO-THREE. *Whee-ee-ee*—there she was in her own kitchen, the umbrella still open in her hand.

'Ee-ee, mother,' said her daughter in astonishment, 'I never saw you come in. How did you get here?'

'I don't rightly know, dearie,' said the poor old lady. 'Make me a cup of tea, will you, love. I feel quite out of breath, I don't know why.'

So she sat down and drank a cup of tea and soon felt quite all right again.

A few days after she went to see her married daughter and, as the sun was shining, she took the magic umbrella with her as a sunshade. After they had washed up after dinner, she and her daughter went to sit by a busy road to watch the cars go by. The farmer's wife was very interested in cars. It was a treat for her to watch them, so she sat down on the grass verge and opened her umbrella to shield her from the sun.

'Eh, what a power of cars there do to be sure,' she said. 'ONE-TWO-THREE-FOUR-FIVE—I wish I were in one of 'em, I do!'

Whee-ee-ee! There she was, sitting in one of the cars on an old lady's lap. The old lady screamed, and her husband stopped the car at the side of the road and said indignantly, 'How dare you jump into my car like that! Get out at once!'

The farmer's wife scrambled out quite bewildered and stood in the middle of the road with the cars streaking by. Her daughter came hurrying up and said, 'Ee-ee, mother! Whatever made you do that?'

'I don't know, dearie,' said the poor old lady, 'I really don't. I think I must be ill. I'd better go to the doctor tomorrow.'

So the next day she and her daughter went to the doctor and, as it was raining, she took the magic umbrella with her. The doctor felt her pulse—*so*—and looked at her tongue—*so*—and said, 'Oh, yes, you've got a touch of Thingumbobitis. You must take these pink pills three times a day, this green medicine five times a day and these blue pills *seven* times a day. Whatever you do, don't let your nose get cold—it would be most dangerous!'

The poor old lady felt quite confused. As she went out of the surgery she said to her daughter, 'Oh dear! I shall never remember all that. What did he say—blue pills three times a day, yellow medicine five times a day, pink pills—how many times had I to take those? ONE-TWO-THREE-FOUR-FIVE-SIX-SEVEN...'

Whee-ee-ee! There she was, floating round and round the church steeple, her umbrella open in her hand like a parachute.

Well—her daughter looked up in amazement. 'Ee-ee!' she said. 'I've never seen my mother do that afore!'

Off she went to the fire station for help and along came the fire engine at full gallop. One by one the firemen set up their long ladders until they reached almost to the top of the steeple. Then while everyone watched in suspense, a fat fireman climbed up and up until he could just reach the old lady's skirts—she was still floating round and round the church steeple. Down, down, down he came, tugging her with him. But just when she was *so* high above the ground, a sudden gust of wind caught the umbrella and blew it away out of sight and the old lady fell to the ground with a bump.

'Ee-ee, mother!' said her daughter, 'whatever made you go up there? I've never seen you do that afore!'

'Eh, I don't know—' said the poor old lady. 'I think I must be really ill. I'd better go to bed.'

And so she did. She stayed there for two whole weeks and she was never ill in that way again. BUT—if *you* should find an umbrella which doesn't belong to you, be careful. You don't want to find yourself floating round and round the church steeple, do you!

Adapted by Eileen Colwell from the story by Rose Fyleman from *Good Morning Tales* (Methuen)
(See Note, page 137)

Fierce Feathers

The sunlight lay in patches on the steep roof of the Meeting-house of Easton Township, in the county of Saratoga, in the State of New York. It was a bright summer morning in the year 1775. The children of Easton Township liked their wooden Meeting-house, although it was made only of rough-hewn logs, nailed hastily together in order to provide some sort of shelter for the worshipping Friends. They would not, if they could, have exchanged it for one of the more stately Meeting-houses at home in England. There, the windows were generally high up in the walls. English children could see nothing through the panes but a peep of sky, or the topmost branches of a tall tree. But out here in America it was very different. To begin with, the logs of the new Meeting-house did not fit quite close together. If a boy or girl happened to be sitting in the corner seat, he or she could often see through a chink right out into the woods. For the untamed wilderness still stretched away on all sides round the newly-cleared settlement of Easton.

Moreover, there were no glass windows in the log house as yet,

12

only open spaces, provided with wooden shutters that could be closed during a summer storm. Another larger open space at the end of the building would be closed by a door when the next cold weather came. At present the summer air blew in softly, laden with the fragrant scents of the flowers and pine-trees. Every now and then a drowsy bee would come blundering in by mistake, and after buzzing about for some time among the assembled Friends, he would make his way out again through one of the chinks between the logs. The children always hoped that a butterfly might also find its way in, some fine day. Especially on a mid-week Meeting like today, they often found it difficult to 'think Meeting thoughts' in the silence or even to attend to what was being said, so busy were they watching for the entrance of that long-desired butterfly.

It was not only the children who found silent worship difficult that still summer morning nearly two hundred years ago. There were signs of anxiety on the faces of many of the Friends and even on the peaceful countenances of the Elders in their raised seats in the gallery. There, at the head of the Meeting, sat Friend Zebulon Hoxie, the grandfather of most of the children who were present. Below him sat his two sons. Opposite them, their wives and families, and a few other Friends. A stranger Friend sat in the gallery that day by their grandfather's side. The children had heard that his name was Robert Nisbet, and that he had walked for two days, thirty miles through the wilderness country, to join the Friends at New Easton at their mid-week Meeting. The children liked his kind, open face and they liked still better the sound of his rich, clear voice that made it easy for even children to listen. But they liked the words of his text best of all: 'The Beloved of the Lord shall dwell in safety by Him. He shall cover them all the day long.'

Robert Nisbet paused a moment as if the words of his message were dear to him, then he went on, 'He shall cover thee with His feathers and under His wings shalt thou trust.' Then he continued: 'You have done well, dear Friends, to stay on valiantly in your homes, when all your neighbours have fled. These

13

promises of covering and shelter are truly meant for you. Make them your own and you shall not be afraid for the terror by night, nor for the arrow that flieth by day.'

The boys and girls on the low benches under the gallery looked at each other. Now they knew what had brought the stranger! He had come because he had heard of the danger that threatened the little clearing of settlers in the woods. For it was just before the outbreak of the Revolutionary War of 1775. The part of the country in which Easton Township was situated was already distressed by visits of scouting parties from both British and American armies, and the American Government, unable to protect the inhabitants, had issued a proclamation directing them to leave the country. This was the reason that all the scattered houses in the neighbourhood were deserted, save only a few tenanted by the handful of Friends.

'You did well, Friends,' the speaker continued, 'well to ask to be permitted to exercise your own judgment without blame to the authorities, well to say to them in all courtesy and charity, "You are clear of us in that you have warned us,"—and to stay on in your dwellings and to carry out your accustomed work. The report of this your courage and faith, hath reached us and the Lord hath charged me to meet with you today, and to bear to you these messages from Him.'

The visitor sat down again in his seat. The furrowed line of anxiety in old Zebulon Hoxie's high forehead smoothed itself away; the eyes of one or two of the younger women filled with tears. As the speaker's voice ceased, little Susannah Hoxie's head, which had been dropping lower and lower, finally found a resting-place, and was encircled by her mother's arm. Young Mrs Hoxie drew off her small daughter's shady hat, and put it on the seat beside her, while she very gently stroked back the golden curls from the child's forehead. In doing this, she caught a rebuking glance from her elder daughter, Dinah.

'Naughty, naughty Susie, to go to sleep in Meeting,' Dinah was thinking; 'it is very hot, and *I* am sleepy too, but *I* don't go to sleep. I do wish a butterfly would come in at the window just

14

for once—or a bird, a little bird with blue and red and pink and yellow feathers. I liked what that stranger Friend said about "being covered with feathers all the day long". I wish I was all covered with feathers. I wish there were feathers in Meeting.' She turned in her corner seat and looked through the slit in the wall—why there *were* feathers close outside the wall of the house, red and yellow and blue and pink!

In the meanwhile her brother, Benjamin Hoxie, on the other low seat opposite the window, was also thinking of the stranger's sermon. 'He said it was a valiant thing to do, to stop on here when all the neighbours have left. I didn't know Friends could do valiant things. I thought only soldiers were valiant. But if a scouting party really did come—if those English scouts suddenly appeared, then even a Quaker boy might have a chance to show that he is not a coward, even if he doesn't fight.' Benjamin's eyes strayed also out of the open window. It was very hot and still in the Meeting-house. Yet the bushes were trembling. How strange that there should be a breeze there and not here!

And then, in her turn, Mrs Hoxie looked up, as her little daughter had done, and saw the same tall feathers creeping above the sill of the open Meeting-house window frame. For just one moment her heart, that usually beat so calmly under her grey Quaker robe, seemed to stand absolutely still. She went white to the lips. Then 'shall dwell in safety by Him,' the words flashed back to her mind. She looked across to where her husband sat— an urgent look. He met her eyes, read them, and followed the direction in which she gazed. Then he, too, saw the feathers— three, five, seven, nine, in a row above the sill. Another instant, and a dark-skinned face appeared beneath them, looking over the sill. The moment most to be dreaded in the lives of all American settlers—more terrible than any visit from civilized soldiers— had come suddenly upon the little company of Friends alone here in the wilderness. An Indian Chief was staring in at the Meeting-house window, showing his teeth in a cruel grin. In his hand he held a sheaf of arrows, poisoned arrows, only too ready to fly, and kill by day.

15

All the assembled Friends were aware of his presence by this time, and were watching the window now, though not one of them moved. Mrs Hoxie glanced towards her other little daughter, and saw to her great relief that Dinah too had fallen asleep, her head against the wooden wall. Dinah and Susie were the two youngest children in Meeting. The others were mostly older even than Benjamin, who was twelve. They were, therefore, too well-trained in Quaker stillness to move for any Indians, until the Friends at the head of the Meeting had shaken hands and given the signal to disperse. Nevertheless, the hearts of even the elder girls were beating fast. Benjamin's lips were tightly shut, and with eyes that were unusually bright he followed every movement of the Indian Chief, who without making the slightest noise had moved round to the open doorway.

There he stood, the naked brown figure, in full war-paint and feathers, looking with piercing eyes at each Friend in turn, as if one of them must have the weapons he sought. But the Friends were entirely unarmed. There was not a gun, or a rifle, or a sword to be found in any of their dwelling-places even, least of all in their peaceful Meeting-house.

A minute later, a dozen other Redskins, equally terrible, stood beside their Chief. The bushes trembled no longer. It was Benjamin who found it hard not to tremble now, as he saw thirteen sharp arrows taken from their quivers and their notches held taut to thirteen bowstrings, all ready to shoot. Yet still the the Friends sat on, without stirring, in complete silence.

Only Benjamin, turning his head to look at his grandfather, saw Zebulon Hoxie, gazing full at the Chief. The Indian's flashing eyes, under the black eyebrows, gazed back fiercely into the Quaker's calm blue eyes beneath the snowy hair. No word was spoken, but in silence two powers were measured against each other—the power of hate and the power of love. For steady friendliness to his strange visitors was written in every line of Zebulon Hoxie's face.

The steadfast gaze lasted for what seemed to be a long time, but at length the Indian's eyes fell. His head that he had carried so haughtily sank towards his breast. He glanced round the Meeting-house with a scrutiny that nothing could escape. Then, at a sign to his followers, the thirteen arrows were noiselessly replaced in thirteen quivers, the thirteen bows were leaned against the wall, many footsteps, lighter than falling snow, crossed the floor. The Indian Chief, unarmed, sat himself down in the nearest seat, with his followers in all their war-paint but also unarmed, close round him.

The Meeting did not stop. It continued—one of the strangest Friends' Meetings, surely, that ever was held. The Meeting not only continued, it increased in solemnity and power.

Never did any of those present that day forget that silent Meeting, or the Presence that closer, clearer than the sunlight, filled the bright room. 'He shall cover thee with His feathers all the day long.'

The Friends sat in their accustomed stillness. But the Indians sat more still than any of them. They seemed strangely at home in the stillness, these wild men of the woods. Motionless they sat, as a group of trees on a windless day; silent, as if they were themselves a part of Nature's own silence rather than of the family of her unquiet, human children. The slow minutes slipped by. The peace grew and deepened.

At last, when the accustomed hour of worship was ended, the two Friends at the head of the Meeting shook hands solemnly. Then, and not till then, did old Zebulon Hoxie advance to the Indian Chief and with signs invite him and his followers to come to his house. With signs they accepted. The strange procession crossed the sunlit path. Susie and Dinah, wide awake now, but silent in obedience to their mother's whispers, watched the Indians' feathers with untroubled eyes that knew no fear.

When the company had arrived at the house, Zebulon put bread and cheese on the table and invited his unusual guests to help themselves. They did so, thanking him with signs. The Chief began to speak in broken English to old Zebulon Hoxie, gesticulating to make his meaning clear.

'Indian come White Man house,' he said, pointing towards

17

the settlement. 'Indian want kill White Man, one, two, three, six, all!' and he clutched the tomahawk at his belt with a gruesome gesture. 'Indian come, see White Man sit in house—no gun, no arrow, no knife. All quiet, all still, worshipping Great Spirit. Great Spirit inside Indian, too,' and he pointed to his breast. 'Then Great Spirit say: "Indian! No kill them!"'

The Chief took a white feather from one of his arrows and placed it firmly over the centre of the roof in a peculiar way. 'With that white feather above house,' he said, 'White Man's house safe. We Indians your friends, you ours.'

A moment later and the strange guests had all disappeared as noiselessly as they had come. But, when the bushes ceased to tremble, Benjamin crept to his mother's side. 'Mother, did you *see*, did you *see*?' he whispered fearfully. 'Did you and father and grandfather not see what those things were, hanging from the Indians' belts? They were scalps—scalps of people they had killed!' and again he shuddered.

His mother stooped and kissed him. 'Yes, my son,' she answered, 'I did see. In truth we all saw, too well. But thou, my son, pray for the slayers as well as the slain. For thyself and us, have no fear. "He shall cover thee with His feathers and under His wings shalt thou trust."'

Adapted by Eileen Colwell from *A Book of Quaker Saints* by L. V. Hodgkin (Friends' Home Service Committee)
(See Note, page 138)

8 › Molly Whuppie

Once upon a time, there was an old woodcutter who had too many children. Work as hard as he might, he couldn't feed them all. So he took the three youngest of them, gave them a last slice of bread and treacle each, and abandoned them in the forest.

They ate the bread and treacle and walked and walked until they were worn out and utterly lost. Soon they would have lain down together like the babes in the wood, and that would have been the end of them if, just as it was beginning to get dark, they had not spied a small and beaming light between the trees. Now this light was chinkling out from a window. So the youngest of them, who was called Molly Whuppie and was by far the cleverest, went and knocked at the door. A woman came to the door and asked them what they wanted. Molly Whuppie said: 'Something to eat.'

'Eat!' said the woman. 'Eat! Why, my husband's a giant, and soon as say knife, he'd eat *you*!'

But they were tired out and famished, and still Molly begged the woman to let them in.

So at last the woman took them in, sat them down by the fire on a billet of wood, and gave them some bread and milk. Hardly had they taken a sup of it when there came a thumping at the door. No mistaking that: it was the giant come home; and in he came.

'Hai!' he said, squinting at the children. 'What have we here?'

'Three poor, cold, hungry, lost little lasses,' said his wife. 'You get to your supper, my man, and leave them to me.'

The giant said nothing, sat down and ate up his supper; but between the bites he looked at the children.

Now the giant had three daughters of his own, and the giant's wife put the whole six of them into the same bed. For so she thought she would keep the strangers safe. But before he went to bed the giant, as if in play, hung three chains of gold round his daughters' necks, and three of golden straw round Molly's and her sisters' between the sheets.

Soon the other five were fast asleep in the great bed, but Molly lay awake listening. At last she rose up softly, and, creeping across, changed over one by one the necklaces of gold and of straw. So now it was Molly and her sisters who wore the chains of gold, and the giant's three daughters the chains of straw. Then she lay down again.

In the middle of the night the giant came tiptoeing into the room, and, groping cautiously with finger and thumb, he plucked up out of the bed the three children with the straw necklaces round their necks, carried them downstairs, and bolted them up in his great cellar.

'So, so, my pretty chickabiddies!' he smiled to himself as he bolted the door. 'Now you're safe!'

As soon as all was quiet again, Molly Whuppie thought it high time she and her sisters were out of that house. So she woke them, whispering in their ears, and they slipped down the stairs together and out into the forest, and never stopped running till morning.

But daybreak came at last, and lo and behold, they came to another house. It stood beside a pool of water full of wild swans, and stone images there, and a thousand windows; and it was the house of the King. So Molly went in, and told her story to the King. The King listened, and when it was finished, said:

'Well, Molly, that's one thing done, and done well. But I could tell another thing, and that would be a better.' This King, indeed, knew the giant of old; and he told Molly that if she would go back and steal for him the giant's sword that hung behind his bed, he would give her eldest sister his eldest son for a husband, and then Molly's sister would be a princess.

Molly looked at the eldest prince, for there they all sat at breakfast, and she smiled and said she would try.

So, that very evening, she muffled herself up, and made her way back through the forest to the house of the giant. First she listened at the window, and there she heard the giant eating his supper; so she crept into the house and hid herself under his bed.

In the middle of the night—and the shutters fairly shook with the giant's snoring—Molly climbed softly up on to the great bed and unhooked the giant's sword that was dangling from its nail in the wall. Lucky it was for Molly this was not the giant's great fighting sword, but only a little sword. It was heavy enough for all that, and when she came to the door, it rattled in its scabbard and woke up the giant.

Then Molly ran, and the giant ran, and they both ran, and at last they came to the Bridge of the One Hair, and Molly ran over. But not the giant; for run over he couldn't. Instead, he shook his fist at her across the chasm in between, and shouted:

> 'Woe betide ye, Molly Whuppie,
> If ye e'er come back again!'

But Molly only laughed and said:

> 'Maybe twice I'll come to see 'ee,
> If so be I come to Spain.'

Then Molly carried off the sword to the King; and her eldest sister married the King's eldest son.

'Well,' said the King, when the wedding was over, 'that was a better thing done, Molly, and done well. But I know another, and that's better still. Steal the purse that lies under the giant's pillow, and I'll marry your second sister to my second son.'

Molly looked at the King's second son, and laughed, and said she would try.

So she muffled herself up in another coloured hood, and stole off through the forest to the giant's house, and there he was, guzzling as usual at supper. This time she hid herself in his linen closet. A stuffy place that was.

About the middle of the night, she crept out of the linen closet, took a deep breath, and pushed in her fingers just a little bit betwixt his bolster and pillow. The giant stopped snoring and sighed, but soon began to snore again. Then Molly slid her fingers in a little bit further under his pillow. At this the giant called out in his sleep as if there were robbers near. And his wife said: 'Lie easy, man! It's those bones you had for supper.'

Then Molly pushed in her fingers even a little bit further, and then they felt the purse. But as she drew out the purse from under the pillow, a gold piece dropped out of it and clanked on to the floor, and at sound of it the giant woke.

Then Molly ran, and the giant ran, and they both ran. And they both ran and ran until they came to the Bridge of the One Hair. And Molly got over, but the giant stayed; for get over he couldn't. Then he cried out on her across the chasm:

> 'Woe betide ye, Molly Whuppie,
> If ye e'er come back again!'

But Molly only laughed, and called back at him:

> 'Once again I'll come to see 'ee,
> If so be I come to Spain.'

So she took the purse to the King, and her second sister married his second son; and there were great rejoicings.

'Well, well,' said the King to Molly, when the feasting was over, 'that was yet a better thing done, Molly, and done for good. But I know a better yet, and that's the best of all. Steal the giant's ring for me from off his thumb, and you shall have my youngest son for yourself. And all solemn, Molly, you were always my favourite.'

Molly laughed and looked at the King's youngest son, turned her head, frowned, then laughed again, and said she would try. This time, when she had stolen into the giant's house, she hid in the chimney niche.

At dead of night, when the giant was snoring, she stepped out of the chimney niche and crept towards the bed. By good chance the giant lay on his back, his head on his pillow, with his arm hanging down out over the bedside, and it was the arm that had the hand at the end of it on which was the great thumb that wore the ring. First Molly wetted the giant's thumb, then she tugged softly and softly at the ring. Little by little it slid down and down over the knuckle-bone; but just as Molly had slipped it off and pushed it into her pocket, the giant woke with a roar, clutched at her, gripped her, and lifted her clean up into the dark over his head.

'Ah-ha! Molly Whuppie!' says he. 'Once too many is never again. Ay, and if *I'd* done the ill to you as the ill you have done's been done to me, what would I be getting for *my* pains?'

'Why,' says Molly all in one breath, 'I'd bundle you up into a sack, and I'd put the cat and dog inside with you, and a needle and thread and a great pair of shears, and I'd hang you up on the wall, be off to the wood, cut the thickest stick I could get, come home, take you down, and beat you to a jelly. *That's* what I'd do!'

'And that, Molly,' says the giant, chuckling to himself with pleasure and pride at his cunning, 'that's just what I will be doing with you.' So he rose up out of his bed and fetched a sack, put Molly into the sack, and the cat and the dog besides, and a needle and thread and a stout pair of shears, and hung her up on the wall. Then away he went into the forest to cut a cudgel.

When he was well gone, Molly, stroking the dog with one

23

hand and the cat with the other, sang out in a high, clear, jubilant voice: 'Oh, if only everybody could see what I can see!'

'"See," Molly?' said the giant's wife. 'What do you see?'

But Molly only said, 'Oh, if only everybody could see what I see! Oh, if only they could see what *I* see!'

At last the giant's wife begged and entreated Molly to take her up into the sack so that she could see what Molly saw. Then Molly took the shears and cut a hole in the lowest corner of the sack, jumped out of the sack, helped the giant's wife up into it, and, as fast as she could, sewed up the hole with the needle and thread.

But it was pitch black in the sack, so the giant's wife saw nothing but stars, and they were inside of her, and she soon began to ask to be let out again. Molly never heeded or answered her, but hid herself far in at the back of the door. Home at last came the giant, with a quickwood cudgel in his hand and a knob at the end of it as big as a pumpkin. And he began to belabour the sack with the cudgel.

His wife cried: 'Stay, man! It's me, man! Oh, man, it's me, man!' But the dog barked and the cat squalled, and at first he didn't hear her voice.

Then Molly crept softly out from behind the door. But the giant saw her. He gave a roar. And Molly ran, and the giant ran, and they both ran, and they ran and they ran and they ran— Molly and the giant—till they came to the Bridge of the One Hair. And Molly skipped along over it; but the giant stayed, for he couldn't. And he cried out after her in a dreadful voice across the chasm:

'Woe betide ye, Molly Whuppie.
If ye e'er come back again!'

But Molly waved her hand at the giant over the chasm, and flung back her head:

'Never again I'll come to see 'ee,
Though so be I come to Spain.'

24

Then Molly ran off with the ring in her pocket, and she was married to the King's youngest son; and there was a feast that was a finer feast than all the feasts that had ever been in the King's house before, and there were lights in all the windows.

Lights so bright that all the dark long the hosts of the wild swans swept circling in space under the stars. But though there were guests by the hundred from all parts of the country, the giant never so much as gnawed a bone!

From *Tales Told Again* by Walter de la Mare (Faber & Faber)
(See Note, page 139)

$10 \rightarrow$ The Death of Balder

Balder was the Sun-god, handsome and gay; Hodur, his twin brother, was the god of darkness, blind and gloomy. When Balder came he brought the sunshine but Hodur brought the dark. All the gods loved Balder, few cared for the melancholy Hodur.

There came a time when Balder lost his cheerful ways and grew pale and sad. Nanna, his wife, was distressed at the change in him. 'What troubles you, dear husband?' she asked.

'Night after night I dream the same terrible dream,' said Balder. 'The air is full of awful warnings. I feel that the last battle of the gods is at hand and darkness and desolation will overwhelm our beautiful world. I dream that someone—I know not who—is doomed to kill me even now and send me to the land of the dead.'

Terrified, Nanna told wise Odin and Frigga of Balder's dream. At once Odin called a council of the gods, for all knew that such dreams boded no good to them or to Balder. How could he be protected from the evil that awaited him?

'We must ask all things in Asgard and on earth to swear not to harm Balder,' they agreed. Frigga herself sent out messengers

26

everywhere to ensure that no one living thing was missed. Fire and water, rocks and metals above and below the earth, plants and trees, birds, animals and insects, even sickness and plague swore that they would never harm Balder. Frigga was happy for now Balder her son must be safe. Only wise Odin still feared that the death of Balder would be the sign that the twilight of the gods was at hand.

One other god was uneasy, but for a very different reason. The evil Loki would have liked the sun to be dimmed for ever and he hated Balder because he was loved so well. Plotting evil in his heart, Loki took the form of an old woman and went to see Frigga.

As he passed through the courtyard of Asgard, the gods were enjoying rare sport. Now that nothing could harm Balder, his friends were amusing themselves casting weapons and stones at him, while he stood smiling and unafraid. Spears turned aside of themselves, stones fell harmlessly, and all things kept their oath to spare Balder.

Loki watched from the back of the laughing crowd, scowling with malice. Presently he slipped away to Frigga and told her of the new sport the gods were enjoying. 'Surely this is dangerous,' said the cunning Loki. 'I would not have the good Balder harmed. Are you sure that *all* things have sworn not to harm him? Perhaps you have forgotten to ask just one thing or one person?'

'Only one thing did not swear,' said Frigga smiling, 'but that was because I did not ask it to do so. What harm could come from the soft and yielding sprig of mistletoe which grows on the oak tree at the gate!'

'What harm indeed!' said Loki, his heart full of triumph. At once he hurried away to the oak tree and tore away the sprig of mistletoe. Then casting aside his disguise, he returned to the courtyard. The gods were still at their sport and Balder was still unharmed. Only Hodur, Balder's blind brother, had not joined in the game for he could not see to aim at Balder.

Loki crept up to him and said falsely, 'It is a shame that you cannot join the sport, Hodur. Let me help you to throw once anyway,' and he put into Hodur's hand a dart made of the mistletoe, and with an evil smile, guided his hand to throw it.

And Hodur, all unwitting, pleased and laughing, threw the tiny dart and pierced his brother through the heart. Without a cry he fell to the ground dead.

There was a sudden silence. The laughter ceased. No one moved. All were stricken with horror and grief. At last Hodur, puzzled by the silence, asked, 'What has happened?' Stretching out his hands before him helplessly, he began to grope his way towards Balder.

'Balder is dead, is dead,' said a hollow voice out of the crowd. 'It is you, his brother, who has killed him. You are accursed for ever.'

Then each man cried aloud in grief for Balder, but Hodur, horror-stricken, stumbled away into the darkness of the forest.

Bitter was Frigga's grief for her son. 'Is there not a brave man who will ride to the realms of the dead?' she pleaded. 'Surely if a ransom is offered to Hel the ruler of the souls of the dead, she will allow Balder to return to us.'

At once Hermod, messenger of the gods, offered to go even to the gates of the underworld for Balder's sake. Mounted on Odin's own horse, Sleipner, he rode away to misty Niflheim.

Nine days he rode until he reached the bridge over the river at the entrance to the kingdom of Hel. There the maiden who guarded the bridge, ordered him to stop. 'Your footsteps shake the earth more than five regiments of the dead,' she said. 'Your face is too bright for death. Why do you ride here?'

'I am Hermod, the messenger of the gods. I seek Balder. Has he passed this way?' asked Hermod.

'Indeed, yes, he is even now in the house of Hel,' said the maiden and allowed him to cross the bridge.

Hermod galloped on. At one bound he leapt over the gate of Hel's palace. Taking no notice of the fearsome hound Garm, he rode through the courtyard with its pale twittering ghosts and into the palace.

There in the throne-room sat Hel and gazed at him coldly. In spite of his courage, Hermod felt terror rise within him. Beside Hel sat Balder and his wife Nanna, for she had died of grief for her husband when she heard of his death. Balder and Nanna were but misty shapes and so pale that they could scarcely be seen in the gloom.

Hermod knelt at the feet of Hel. 'Name a ransom for Balder,' he implored, 'and however large, it shall be paid gladly, for all men mourn Balder dead.'

There was silence and then Hel answered in her harsh voice. 'He shall return if all things indeed weep for him. If one thing, one person, refuse to weep, then he is mine for ever.'

Joyfully Hermod sprang to his feet and greeted pale Balder. 'May we soon meet again in joy!' he cried. Swiftly he rode away on Sleipner, back to Asgard and to life.

When the gods heard of the ransom asked for Balder, they too rejoiced. 'Surely no one and no thing will refuse to weep for Balder, our Sun-god!' they said confidently. Messengers sped willingly north and south, east and west, and everywhere there was weeping for Balder. Great trees sighed, the wind wailed through their branches, flowers wept for the warmth that came from Balder to bring them into blossom, the sound of weeping filled every corner of earth and heaven.

Triumphantly the messengers sped back to Asgard. On the way, however, they saw a cave which they had not seen before and entered it to find whether there was any living thing within. There sat a hideous giantess, Thökk.

'Weep, Thökk,' they said, 'weep for Balder, for surely you are the only living thing that has not shed tears for him.'

'Why should I weep for Balder?' said Thökk with a cruel laugh. 'I care nothing for Balder. Let Hel keep him!' Angrily the messengers started forward to seize Thökk, but she had vanished. They could do nothing.

Sadly they returned to Asgard and told their tale. Now there was no hope for the return of the bright Sun-god. Thökk—whom many believed to be Loki in disguise—had condemned Balder to dwell in the land of the dead for ever.

Weeping, the gods carried the bodies of Balder and his wife to the edge of the sea and laid them on Balder's own ship Ringhorn. A shadow rose out of the deep and spread over heaven and earth and in that shadow the grim mountain giants watched in a dark menacing circle. Balder's armour was placed at his feet together with many gifts. In the presence of gods and men, Odin lit the bale-fire with a flaming torch and stood back, his ravens flying about his head.

The blazing ship was pushed from the shore and drifted out to sea, the flames growing fainter and fainter until all was dark. Balder the Beautiful was lost to the world for ever and with him went the sun.

Neither did blind Hodur live long, for soon he met his death at the hands of Vali, the appointed avenger. Weary and sad he left this life, but in the land of the dead his brother received him in love and kindness.

Thus did all things come to pass as decreed.

Adapted by Eileen Colwell from Barbara Leonie Picard's version in
Tales from the Norse Gods and Heroes
(Oxford University Press)
(See Note, page 140)

A Woman sat by the Churchyard Door

A woman sat by the churchyard door,
Chorus: Ooh-ooh-ooh-ooh, aah-aah-aah-aah,

Nobody'd ever sat there before,
Chorus: Ooh-ooh-ooh-ooh, aah-aah-aah-aah,

Three ghosties came and sat down near,
Chorus: Ooh-ooh-ooh-ooh, aah-aah-aah-aah,

The old woman shook with fright and fear,
Chorus: Ooh-ooh-ooh-ooh, aah-aah-aah-aah,

The old woman to the ghosties said,
Chorus: Ooh-ooh-ooh-ooh, aah-aah-aah-aah,

'Will I be like you when I'm dead?'
Chorus: Ooh-ooh-ooh-ooh, aah-aah-aah-aah,

The ghosties to the woman said,
Chorus: *'AAAAAAAAAAAAAAAAA*
AAAAAH!'
(loud scream)

Traditional
(See Note, page 141)

The Elephant's Picnic

Elephants are generally clever animals, but there was once an elephant who was very silly; and his great friend was a kangaroo. Now, kangaroos are not often clever animals, and this one certainly was not, so she and the elephant got on very well together.

One day they thought they would like to go off for a picnic by themselves. But they did not know anything about picnics, and had not the faintest idea of what to do to get ready.

'What do you do on a picnic?' the elephant asked a child he knew.

'Oh, we collect wood and make a fire, and then we boil the kettle,' said the child.

'What do you boil the kettle for?' said the elephant in surprise.

'Why, for tea, of course,' said the child in a snapping sort of way; so the elephant did not like to ask any more questions. But he went and told the kangaroo, and they collected together all the things they thought they would need.

When they got to the place where they were going to have their picnic, the kangaroo said that she would collect the wood because she had got a pouch to carry it back in. A kangaroo's pouch, of

32

course, is very small; so the kangaroo carefully chose the smallest twigs she could find, and only about five or six of those. In fact, it took a lot of hopping to find any sticks small enough to go in her pouch at all; and it was a long time before she came back. But silly though the elephant was, he soon saw those sticks would not be enough for a fire.

'Now *I* will go off and get some wood,' he said.

His ideas of getting wood were very different. Instead of taking little twigs he pushed down whole trees with his forehead, and staggered back to the picnic-place with them rolled up in his trunk. Then the kangaroo struck a match, and they lit a bonfire made of whole trees. The blaze, of course, was enormous, and the fire so hot that for a long time they could not get near it; and it was not until it began to die down a bit that they were able to get near enough to cook anything.

'Now let's boil the kettle,' said the elephant. Amongst the things he had brought was a brightly shining copper kettle and a very large black iron saucepan. The elephant filled the saucepan with water.

'What are you doing that for?' said the kangaroo.

'To boil the kettle in, you silly,' said the elephant. So he popped the kettle in the saucepan of water, and put the saucepan on the fire; for he thought, the old juggins, that you boil a kettle in the same sort of way you boil an egg, or boil a cabbage! And the kangaroo, of course, did not know any better.

So they boiled and boiled the kettle, and every now and then they prodded it with a stick.

'It doesn't seem to be getting tender,' said the elephant sadly, 'and I'm sure we can't eat it for tea until it does.'

So then away he went and got more wood for the fire; and still the saucepan boiled and boiled, and still the kettle remained as hard as ever. It was getting late now, almost dark.

'I am afraid it won't be ready for tea,' said the kangaroo. 'I am afraid we shall have to spend the night here. I wish we had got something with us to sleep in.'

'Haven't you?' said the elephant. 'You mean to say you

33

didn't pack before you came away?'

'No,' said the kangaroo. 'What should I have packed, anyway?'

'Why, your trunk, of course,' said the elephant. 'That is what people pack.'

'But I haven't got a trunk,' said the kangaroo.

'Well, I have,' said the elephant, 'and I've packed it. Kindly pass the pepper; I want to unpack!'

So then the kangaroo passed the elephant the pepper, and the elephant took a good sniff. Then he gave a most enormous sneeze, and everything he had packed in his trunk shot out of it—tooth-brush, spare socks, gym shoes, a comb, a bag of bull's eyes, his pyjamas, and his Sunday suit. So then the elephant put on his pyjamas and lay down to sleep; but the kangaroo had no pyjamas, and so, of course, she could not possibly sleep.

'All right,' she said to the elephant; 'you sleep and I will sit up and keep the fire going.'

So all night the kangaroo kept the fire blazing brightly and the kettle boiling merrily in the saucepan. When the next morning came the elephant woke up.

'Now,' he said, 'let's have our breakfast.'

So they took the kettle out of the saucepan; and what do you think? *It was boiled as tender as tender could be!* So they cut it fairly in half and shared it between them, and ate it for their breakfast; and both agreed they had never had so good a breakfast in their lives.

From *Don't Blame Me and other Stories* by Richard Hughes (Chatto & Windus) (See Note, page 142)

The Woman of the Sea

One clear summer night, a young man was walking on the sand by the sea on the Isle of Unst. He had been all day in the hayfields and was come down to the shore to cool himself, for it was the full of the moon and the wind blowing fresh off the water.

As he came to the shore he saw the sand shining white in the moonlight and on it the sea-people dancing. He had never seen them before, for they show themselves like seals by day, but on this night, because it was midsummer and a full moon, they were dancing for joy. Here and there he saw dark patches where they had flung down their sealskins, but they themselves were as clear as the moon itself, and they cast no shadow.

He crept a little nearer, and his own shadow moved before him, and all of a sudden one of the sea-people danced upon it. The dance was broken. They looked about and saw him and with

35

a cry they fled to their sealskins and dived into the waves. The air was full of their soft crying and splashing.

But one of the fairy-people ran hither and thither on the sands, wringing her hands as if she had lost something. The young man looked and saw a patch of darkness in his own shadow. It was a seal's skin. Quickly he threw it behind a rock and watched to see what the sea-fairy would do.

She ran down to the edge of the sea and stood with her white feet in the foam, crying to her people to wait for her, but they had gone too far to hear. The moon shone on her and the young man thought she was the loveliest creature he had ever seen. Then she began to weep softly to herself and the sound of it was so pitiful that he could bear it no longer. He stood upright and went down to her.

'What have you lost, woman of the sea?' he asked her.

She turned at the sound of his voice and looked at him, terrified. For a moment he thought she was going to dive into the sea. Then she came a step nearer and held up her two hands to him.

'Sir,' she said, 'give it back to me and I and my people will give you the treasure of the sea.' Her voice was like the waves singing in a shell.

'I would rather have you than the treasure of the sea,' said the young man. Although she hid her face in her hands and fell again to crying, more hopelessly than ever, he was not moved.

'It is my wife you shall be,' he said. 'Come with me now to the priest, and we will go home to our own house, and it is yourself shall be the mistress of all I have. It is warm you will be in the long winter nights, sitting at your own hearth stone and the peat burning red, instead of swimming in the cold green sea.'

She tried to tell him of the bottom of the sea where there comes neither snow nor darkness of night and the waves are as warm as a river in summer, but he would not listen. Then he threw his cloak around her and lifted her in his arms and they were married in the priest's house.

He brought her home to his little thatched cottage and into the kitchen with its earthen floor, and set her down before the hearth in the red glow of the peat. She cried out when she saw the fire, for she thought it was a strange crimson jewel.

'Have you anything as bonny as that in the sea?' he asked her, kneeling down beside her and she said, so faintly that he could scarcely hear her, 'No'.

'I know not what there is in the sea,' he said, 'but there is nothing on land as bonny as you.' For the first time she ceased her crying and sat looking into the heart of the fire. It was the first thing that made her forget, even for a moment, the sea which was her home.

All the days she was in the young man's house, she never lost the wonder of the fire and it was the first thing she brought her children to see. For she had three children in the twice seven years she lived with him. She was a good wife to him. She baked his bread and she spun the wool from the fleece of his Shetland sheep.

He never named the seal's skin to her, nor she to him, and he thought she was content, for he loved her dearly and she was happy with her children. Once, when he was ploughing on the headland above the bay, he looked down and saw her standing on the rocks and crying in a mournful voice to a great seal in the water. He said nothing when he came home, for he thought to himself it was not to wonder at if she were lonely for a sight of her own people. As for the seal's skin, he had hidden it well.

There came a September evening and she was busy in the house, and the children playing hide-and-seek in the stacks in the gloaming. She heard them shouting and went out to them.

'What have you found?' she said.

The children came running to her. 'It is like a big cat,' they said, 'but it is softer than a cat. Look!' She looked and saw her seal's skin that was hidden under last year's hay.

She gazed at it, and for a long time she stood still. It was warm dusk and the air was yellow with the afterglow of the sunset. The children had run away again, and their voices among the stacks sounded like the voices of birds. The hens were on the roost already and now and then one of them clucked in its sleep. The air was full of little friendly noises from the sleepy talking of the swallows under the thatch. The door was open and the warm smell of the baking of bread came out to her.

She turned to go in, but a small breath of wind rustled over the stacks and she stopped again. It brought a sound that she had heard so long she never seemed to hear it at all. It was the sea whispering down on the sand. Far out on the rocks the great waves broke in a boom, and close in on the sand the little waves slipped racing back. She took up the seal's skin and went swiftly down the track that led to the sands. The children saw her and cried to her to wait for them, but she did not hear them. She was just out of sight when their father came in from the byre and they ran to tell him.

'Which road did she take?' said he.

'The low road to the sea,' they answered, but already their father was running to the shore. The children tried to follow him, but their voices died away behind him, so fast did he run.

As he ran across the hard sands, he saw her dive to join the big seal who was waiting for her, and he gave a loud cry to stop her. For a moment she rested on the surface of the sea, then she cried with her voice that was like the waves singing in a shell, 'Fare ye well, and all good befall you, for you were a good man to me.'

Then she dived to the fairy places that lie at the bottom of the sea and the big seal with her.

For a long time her husband watched for her to come back to him and the children; but she came no more.

Edited by Eileen Colwell from *The Princess Splendour and Other Stories* by Helen Waddell (Longman Young Books)
(See note, page 142)

10 →

A Girl Calling

Once upon a time
when the snow was falling
a girl went calling
from tree to tree:
My dove,
where can he be?
I have lost my soft-winged dove
with eyes of jet
and coral feet,
I have lost my love,
my pet,
my sweet.
Every day
he brought me a gold nut
from the filbert-tree
of the fairy king,
every day
inside the nut was shut
a present for me,

a toy, a ring,
a something, a nothing, an anything.
It kept me glad all day.
But now the ice-cold
wizard
who lives in the blizzard
has driven my dove away,
driven my dove away.
There will no gold
nut
with a secret shut
inside its shell
till the snow has lifted its spell,
and my sweet
with the eyes of jet,
my pet
with the coral feet,
my love
with the soft white wing,
my dove
flies back in the spring.
So through the falling
snow, the girl went calling,
calling . . . calling
from tree to tree:
my love,
my love,
my dove,
where can he be?

From *Silver Sand and Snow*
by Eleanor Farjeon
(Michael Joseph)
(See Note, page 143)

Stan Bolovan

8-11

Once upon a time what happened did happen, and if it had not happened this story would never have been told. On the outskirts of a village, just where the oxen were turned out to pasture, and the pigs roamed about, burrowing with their noses among the roots of the trees, there stood a small house. In the house lived a man who had a wife, and the wife was sad all day long.

'Dear wife, what is wrong with you that you hang your head like a drooping rosebud?' asked her husband one morning. 'You have everything you want; why cannot you be merry like other women?'

'Leave me alone and do not seek to know the reason,' replied his wife, bursting into tears, and the man thought it was no time to question her and went away to his work.

He could not, however, forget all about it, and a few days later he asked again the reason of her sadness, only to be given the same reply. At length he felt he could bear it no longer and tried a third time, and then his wife answered him.

'Good gracious!' cried she. 'Why cannot you let things be as they are? If I were to tell you, you would become just as wretched as myself. If you would only believe it, it is far better for you to know nothing.'

But no man yet was ever content with such an answer. The more you beg him not to inquire, the greater is his curiosity to learn the whole.

'Well, if you must know,' said the wife at last, 'I will tell you. There is no luck in this house—no luck at all!'

'Is not your cow the best milker in all the village? Are not your trees as full of fruit as your hives are full of bees? Has anyone cornfields like ours? Really, you talk nonsense when you say things like that!'

41

'Yes, all that you say is true, but we have no children.'

Then Stan understood, and, when a man once understands and has his eyes opened, it is no longer well with him. From that day the little house on the outskirts contained an unhappy man as well as an unhappy woman. And at the sight of her husband's misery the woman became more wretched than ever.

And so matters went on for some time.

Weeks passed, and Stan thought he would consult a wise man who lived a day's journey from his own house. The wise man was sitting before his door when he came up and Stan fell on his knees before him.

'Give me children, my lord, give me children.'

'Take care what you are asking,' replied the wise man. 'Will not children be a burden to you? Are you rich enough to feed and clothe them?'

'Only give them to me, my lord, and I will manage somehow!' And at a sign from the wise man Stan went his way.

He reached home that evening tired and dusty but with hope in his heart. As he drew near his house a sound of voices struck upon his ear and he looked up to see the whole place full of children. Children in the garden, children in the yard, children looking out of every window—it seemed to the man as if all the children in the world must be gathered there. And none was bigger than the other, but each was smaller than the other, and every one was more noisy and more impudent and more daring than the rest. Stan gazed and grew cold with horror as he realized that they all belonged to him.

'Good gracious! How many there are! How many!' he muttered to himself.

'Oh, but not one too many.' His wife smiled, coming up with a crowd of more children clinging to her skirts.

But even she found that it was not so easy to look after a hundred children. And when a few days had passed and they had eaten up all the food there was in the house, they began to cry, 'Father! I am hungry—I am hungry,' till Stan scratched his head and wondered what he was to do next.

It was not that he thought there were too many children, for his life had seemed more full of joy since they appeared, but now it came to the point he did not know how he was to feed them. The cow had ceased to give milk and it was too early for the fruit trees to ripen.

'Do you know, old woman,' said he one day to his wife, 'I must go out into the world and try to bring back food somehow, though I cannot tell where it is to come from.'

To the hungry man any road is long, and then there was always the thought that he had to satisfy a hundred greedy children as well as himself.

Stan wandered and wandered and wandered, till he reached the end of the world, where that which is, is mingled with that which is not. There he saw, a little way off, a sheepfold, with seven sheep in it. In the shadow of some trees lay the rest of the flock.

Stan crept into hiding, hoping that at nightfall he might manage to decoy some of the sheep away and drive them home for food for his family. But he found this could not be done. For at midnight there was a rushing noise, and through the air flew a dragon who drove away a ram, a sheep and a lamb and three fine cattle that were lying close by. And besides these he took the milk of seventy-seven sheep and carried it home to his old mother that she might bathe in it and grow young again. And this happened every night.

The shepherd of the flock bewailed his loss in vain; the dragon only laughed, and Stan saw that this was not the place to get food for his family. But though he quite understood that it was almost hopeless to fight against such a powerful monster, yet the thought of the hungry children at home clung to him like a burr and would not be shaken off.

At last he said to the shepherd, 'What will you give me if I rid you of the dragon?'

'One of every three rams, one of every three sheep, one of every three lambs,' answered the herdsman.

'It is a bargain,' replied Stan, though at the moment he did not know how, supposing he did come off the victor, he would ever be able to drive so large a flock home. However, that matter could be settled later. At present night was not far off and he must consider how best to fight with the dragon.

Just at midnight, a horrible feeling that was new and strange to him came over Stan—a feeling that he could not put into words even to himself, but which almost forced him to give up the battle and take the shortest road home again. He started; then he remembered the children and turned back.

'You or I,' said Stan to himself, and took up his position on the edge of the flock.

'Stop!' he suddenly cried, as the air was filled with a rushing noise and the dragon came dashing past.

'Dear me!' exclaimed the dragon, looking round. 'Who are you, and where do you come from?'

'I am Stan Bolovan, who eats rocks all night and in the day feeds on the flowers of the mountain. If you meddle with those sheep I will carve a cross on your back.'

When the dragon heard these words he stood quite still in the middle of the road, for he knew he had met his match.

'But you will have to fight me first,' he said in a trembling voice, for when you faced him properly the dragon was not brave at all.

'I fight you?' replied Stan. 'Why, I could slay you with one breath!' Then, stooping to pick up a large cheese which lay at his feet, he added, 'Go and get a stone like this out of the river so we may lose no time in seeing who is the better man.'

The dragon did as Stan bade him and brought back a stone out of the brook.

'Can you get buttermilk out of your stone?' asked Stan.

The dragon picked up his stone with one hand and squeezed it till it fell into powder, but no buttermilk flowed from it. 'Of course I can't!' he said angrily.

'Well, if you can't, I can,' answered Stan, and he pressed the cheese till buttermilk flowed through his fingers.

When the dragon saw that, he thought it was time he made the best of his way home again, but Stan stood in his path.

'We have still some accounts to settle,' said he, 'about what you have been doing here.' And the poor dragon was too frightened to stir, lest Stan should slay him at one breath and bury him among the flowers in the mountain pastures.

'Listen to me,' he said at last, 'I see you are a very useful person and my mother has need of a fellow like you. Suppose you enter her service for three days, which are as long as one of your years, and she will pay you each day seven sacks full of ducats.'

Three times seven sacks full of ducats! The offer was very tempting and Stan could not resist it. He did not waste words, but nodded to the dragon, and they started along the road.

It was a long, long way, but when they came to the end they found the dragon's mother, who was as old as time itself, expecting them. Stan saw her eyes shining like lamps from afar, and when they entered the house they beheld a huge kettle standing on the fire, filled with milk. When the old mother found that her son had arrived empty-handed she grew very angry, and fire and flame darted from her nostrils, but before she could speak the dragon turned to Stan.

'Stay here,' said he, 'and wait for me. I am going to explain things to my mother.'

Stan was already repenting bitterly that he had ever come to such a place, but since he was there, there was nothing for it but to take everything quietly and not show that he was afraid.

'Listen, mother,' said the dragon as soon as they were alone, 'I have brought this man in order to get rid of him. He is a terrific fellow who eats rocks and can press buttermilk out of a stone.' And he told her all that had happened the night before.

'Oh, just leave him to me!' said the dragon's mother. 'I have never yet let a man slip through my fingers.' So Stan had to stay and do her service.

The next day she told him that he and her son should try which was the stronger, and she took down a huge club, bound seven times with iron.

The dragon picked it up as if it had been a feather, and after whirling it round his head, flung it lightly three miles away, telling Stan to beat that if he could.

They walked to the spot where the club lay. Stan stooped and felt it; then a great fear came over him, for he knew that he and all his children together would never lift that club from the ground.

'What are you doing?' asked the dragon.

'I was thinking what a beautiful club it was and what a pity it is that it should cause your death.'

'How do you mean—my death?' asked the dragon.

'Only that I am afraid that if I throw it you will never see another dawn. You don't know how strong I am.'

'Oh, never mind that; be quick and throw.'

'If you are really in earnest, let us go and feast for three days: that will at any rate give you three extra days of life.'

Stan spoke so calmly that this time the dragon began to be a little frightened, though he did not quite believe that things could be as bad as Stan said.

They returned to the house, took all the food that could be found in the old mother's larder, and carried it back to the place where the club was lying. Then Stan seated himself on the sack of provisions and remained quietly watching the setting moon.

'What are you doing?' asked the dragon.

'Waiting till the moon gets out of my way.'

'What do you mean? I don't understand.'

'Don't you see that the moon is exactly in my way? But, of course, if you like, I will throw the club into the moon.'

At these words the dragon grew uncomfortable for the second time. He prized the club, which had been left him by his grandfather, very highly, and had no desire that it should be lost in the moon.

'I'll tell you what,' he said, after thinking a little. 'Don't throw the club at all. I will throw it a second time and that will do just as well.'

'No, certainly not!' replied Stan. 'Just wait till the moon sets.'

But the dragon, in dread lest Stan should fulfill his threats, tried what bribes could do, and in the end had to promise Stan seven sacks of ducats before he was suffered to throw back the club himself.

'Oh, dear me, that is indeed a strong man,' said the dragon, turning to his mother. 'Would you believe that I have had the greatest difficulty in preventing him from throwing the club into the moon?'

Then the old woman grew afraid too. Only to think of it! It was no joke to throw things into the moon! So no more was heard of the club, and the next day they all had something else to think about.

'Go and fetch me water!' said the mother, when the morning broke, and gave them twelve buffalo skins with the order to keep filling them till night.

They set out at once for the brook, and in the twinkling of an eye the dragon had filled the whole twelve, carried them into the house, and brought them back to Stan. Stan was tired; he could scarcely lift the buckets when they were empty and he shuddered to think of what would happen when they were full. But he only took an old knife out of his pocket and began to scratch up the earth near the brook.

'What are you doing there? How are you going to carry the water into the house?' asked the dragon.

'How? Dear me, that is easy enough! I shall just take the brook!'

At these words the dragon's jaw dropped. This was the last thing that had ever entered his head, for the brook had been as it was since the days of his grandfather.

'I'll tell you what,' he said. 'Let me carry the skins for you.'

'Most certainly not,' answered Stan, going on with his digging. The dragon, in dread lest he should fulfill his threat, tried what bribes would do, and in the end had again to promise seven sacks of ducats before Stan would agree to leave the brook alone and let the dragon carry the water into the house.

On the third day the old mother sent Stan into the forest for wood and, as usual, the dragon went with him. Before you could count three he had pulled up more trees than Stan could have cut down in a lifetime, and had arranged them neatly in rows. When the dragon had finished, Stan began to look about him and, choosing the biggest tree, he climbed up it and, breaking off a long rope of wild vine, bound the top of the tree to the one next to it. And so he did to a whole line of trees.

'What are you doing there?' asked the dragon.

'You can see for yourself,' answered Stan, going quietly on with his work.

'Why are you tying the trees together?'

'Not to give myself unnecessary work; when I pull up one, all the others will come up too.'

'But how will you carry them home?'

'Dear me! Don't you understand that I am going to take the whole forest back with me?' said Stan, tying two other trees as he spoke.

'I'll tell you what,' cried the dragon, trembling with fear at the thought of such a thing, 'Let me carry the wood for you and you shall have seven times seven sacks full of ducats.'

'You are a good fellow and I agree to your proposal,' answered Stan, and the dragon carried the wood.

Now the three days' service, which were to be reckoned as a year, were over, and the only thing that disturbed Stan was how to get all those ducats back to his home.

In the evening the dragon and his mother had a long talk, but Stan heard every word through a crack in the ceiling.

'Woe be to us, mother,' said the dragon. 'This man will soon get us into his power. Give him his money, and let us be rid of him.'

But the old mother was fond of money, and did not like this. 'Listen to me,' said she, 'you must kill him this very night.'

'I am afraid,' answered the dragon.

'There is nothing to fear,' replied the old mother. 'When he is asleep take the club and hit him on the head with it. It is easily done.'

And so it would have been, had not Stan heard all about it. When the dragon and his mother had put out their lights, he took the pigs' trough and filled it with earth, placed it in his bed, and covered it with clothes. Then he hid himself underneath, and began to snore loudly.

Very soon the dragon stole softly into the room and gave a tremendous blow on the spot where Stan's head should have been. Stan groaned loudly from under the bed, and the dragon went away as softly as he had come. Directly he had closed the door, Stan lifted out the trough and lay down himself, after making everything clean and tidy, but he was wise enough not to shut his eyes that night.

The next morning he came into the room where the dragon and his mother were having breakfast. 'Good morning,' said he.

'Good morning. How did you sleep?'

'Oh, very well, but I dreamed that a flea had bitten me and I seem to feel it still.'

The dragon and his mother looked at each other. 'Do you hear that?' whispered he. 'He talks of a flea. I broke my club on his head.'

This time the mother was as frightened as her son. There was nothing to be done with a man like this, and she made all haste to fill the sacks with ducats, to be rid of Stan as soon as possible. But on his side Stan was trembling like an aspen, for he could not lift even one sack from the ground. So he stood still and looked at them.

'What are you standing there for?' asked the dragon.

'Oh, I was standing here because it has just occurred to me that I should like to stay in your service for another year. I am ashamed that when I get home they should see I have brought back so little. I know that they will cry out, "Just look at Stan Bolovan, who in one year has grown as weak as a dragon."'

Here a shriek of dismay was heard from both the dragon and his mother, who declared they would give him seven or even seven times seven the number of sacks if he would only go away.

'I'll tell you what,' said Stan at last. 'I see you don't want me to stay and I should be very sorry to make myself disagreeable. I will go at once, but only on condition that you shall carry the money home yourself that I may not be put to shame before my friends.'

The words were hardly out of his mouth before the dragon had snatched up the sacks and piled them on his back. Then he and Stan set forth.

The way, though really not far, was yet too long for Stan, but at length he heard his children's voices, and stopped short. He did not wish the dragon to know where he lived, lest some day he should come to take back his treasure. Was there nothing he could say to get rid of the monster? Suddenly an idea came into Stan's head, and he turned round.

'I hardly know what to do,' said he. 'I have a hundred children and I am afraid they may do you harm, for they are always ready for a fight. However, I will do my best to protect you.'

A hundred children! That was indeed no joke! The dragon let fall the sacks from terror and then picked them up again. But the children, who had had nothing to eat since their father had left them, came rushing toward him, waving knives in their right hands and forks in their left, and crying,

'Give us dragon's flesh! We will have dragon's flesh!'

At this dreadful sight the dragon waited no longer. He flung down his sacks where he stood and took flight as fast as he could, so terrified at the fate that awaited him that from that day he has never dared to show his face in the world again.

From *The Violet Fairy Book* by Andrew Lang, adapted by Mrs Lang from *Rumänische Märchen*
(See Note, page 144)

Rocking-Horse Land

Little Prince Freedling woke up with a jump, and sprang out of bed into the sunshine. He was five years old that morning, by all the clocks and calendars in the kingdom; and the day was going to be beautiful. Every golden minute was precious. He was dressed and out of the room before the attendants knew that he was awake.

In the ante-chamber stood piles on piles of glittering presents; when he walked among them they came up to the measure of his waist. His fairy godmother had sent him a toy with the most humorous effect. It was labelled, 'Break me and I shall turn into something else.' So every time he broke it he got a new toy more beautiful than the last. It began by being a hoop, and from that it ran on, while the Prince broke it incessantly for the space of one hour, during which it became by turn—a top, a Noah's ark, a skipping-rope, a man-of-war, a box of bricks, a picture puzzle, a pair of stilts, a drum, a trumpet, a kaleidoscope, a steam-engine, and nine hundred and fifty other things exactly. Then he began to grow discontented, because it would never turn into the same thing again; and after having broken the man-of-war he wanted to get it back again. Also he wanted to see if the steam-engine would go inside the Noah's ark; but the toy would never be two things at the same time either. This was very unsatisfactory. He thought his fairy godmother ought to have sent him two toys, out of which he could make combinations.

At last he broke it once more, and it turned into a kite; and while he was flying the kite he broke the string, and the kite went sailing away up into the nasty blue sky, and was never heard of again.

Then Prince Freedling sat down and howled at his fairy godmother; what a dissembling lot fairy godmothers were, to be

51

sure! They were always setting traps to make their god-children unhappy. Nevertheless, when told to, he took up his pen and wrote her a nice little note, full of bad spelling and tarradiddles, to say what a happy birthday he was spending in breaking up the beautiful toy she had sent him.

Then he went to look at the rest of the presents, and found it quite refreshing to break a few that did not send him giddy by turning into anything else.

Suddenly his eyes became fixed with delight; alone, right at the end of the room, stood a great black rocking-horse. The saddle and bridle were hung with tiny gold bells and balls of coral; and the horse's tail and mane flowed till they almost touched the ground.

The Prince scampered across the room, and threw his arms around the beautiful creature's neck. All its bells jingled as the head swayed gracefully down; and the prince kissed it between the eyes. Great eyes they were, the colour of fire, so wonderfully bright, it seemed they must be really alive, only they did not move, but gazed continually with a set stare at the tapestry-hung walls on which were figures of armed knights riding to battle.

So Prince Freedling mounted to the back of his rocking-horse; and all day long he rode and shouted to the figures of the armed knights, challenging them to fight, or leading them against the enemy.

At length, when it came to be bedtime, weary of so much glory, he was lifted down from the saddle and carried away to bed.

In his sleep Freedling still felt his black rocking-horse swinging to and fro under him, and heard the melodious chime of its bells, and, in the land of dreams, saw a great country open before him, full of the sound of the battle-cry and the hunting-horn calling him to strange perils and triumphs.

In the middle of the night he grew softly awake, and his heart was full of love for his black rocking-horse. He crept gently out of bed: he would go and look at it where it was standing so grand and still in the next room, to make sure it was all safe and not afraid of being by itself in the dark night. Parting the door-hangings he passed through into the wide hollow chamber beyond, all littered about with toys.

The moon was shining in through the window, making a square cistern of light upon the floor. And then, all at once, he saw that the rocking-horse had moved from the place where he had left it! It had crossed the room, and was standing close to the window, with its head toward the night, as though watching the movement of the clouds and the trees swaying in the wind.

The Prince could not understand how it had been moved so; he was a little bit afraid, and stealing timidly across, he took hold of the bridle to comfort himself with the jangle of its bells. As he came close, and looked up into the dark solemn face he saw that the eyes were full of tears, and reaching up felt one fall warm against his hand.

'Why do you weep, my Beautiful?' said the Prince.

The rocking-horse answered, 'I weep because I am a prisoner, and not free. Open the window, Master, and let me go!'

'But if I let you go I shall lose you,' said the Prince. 'Cannot you be happy here with me?'

'Let me go,' said the horse, 'for my brothers call me out of Rocking-Horse Land; I hear my mare whinnying to her foals; and they all cry, seeking me through the ups and hollows of my native fastnesses! Sweet Master, let me go this night, and I will return to you when it is day!'

Then Freedling said, 'How shall I know that you will return: and what name shall I call you by?'

And the rocking-horse answered, 'My name is Rollonde. Search my mane till you find in it a white hair; draw it out and wind it upon one of your fingers; and so long as you have it so wound you are my master; and wherever I am I must return at your bidding.'

So the Prince drew down the rocking-horse's head, and searching the mane, he found the white hair, and wound it upon his finger and tied it. Then he kissed Rollonde between the eyes, saying, 'Go, Rollonde, since I love you, and wish you to be happy;

only return to me when it is day!' And so saying, he threw open the window to the stir of the night.

Then the rocking-horse lifted his dark head and neighed aloud for joy, and swaying forward with a mighty circling motion rose full into the air, and sprang out into the free world before him.

Freedling watched how with plunge and curve he went over the bowed trees; and again he neighed into the darkness of the night, then swifter than wind he disappeared in the distance. And faintly from far away came a sound of the neighing of many horses answering him.

Then the Prince closed the window and crept back to bed; and all night long he dreamed strange dreams of Rocking-Horse Land. There he saw smooth hills and valleys that rose and sank without a stone or a tree to disturb the steel-like polish of their surface, slippery as glass, and driven over by a strong wind; and over them, with a sound like the humming of bees, flew the rocking-horses. Up and down, up and down, with bright manes streaming like coloured fires, and feet motionless behind and before, went the swift pendulum of their flight. Their long bodies bowed and rose; their heads worked to give impetus to their going; they cried, neighing to each other over hill and valley, 'Which of us shall be first? which of us shall be first?' After them the mares with their tall foals came spinning to watch, crying also among themselves, 'Ah! which shall be first?'

'Rollonde, Rollonde is first!' shouted the Prince, clapping his hands as they reached the goal; and at that, all at once, he woke and saw it was broad day. Then he ran and threw open the window, and holding out the finger that carried the white hair, cried, 'Rollonde, Rollonde, come back, Rollonde!'

Far away he heard an answering sound; and in another moment there came the great rocking-horse himself, dipping and dancing over the hills. He crossed the woods and cleared the palace-wall at a bound, and floating in through the window, dropped to rest at Prince Freedling's side, rocking gently to and fro as though panting from the strain of his long flight.

'Now are you happy?' asked the Prince as he caressed him. 'Ah! sweet Prince,' said Rollonde, 'ah, kind Master!' And then he said no more, but became the still staring rocking-horse of the day before, with fixed eyes and rigid limbs, which could do nothing but rock up and down with a jangling of sweet bells so long as the Prince rode him.

That night Freedling came again when all was still in the palace; and now as before Rollonde had moved from his place and was standing with his head against the window waiting to be let out. 'Ah, dear Master,' he said, so soon as he saw the Prince coming, 'let me go this night also, and surely I will return with day.'

So again the Prince opened the window, and watched him disappear, and heard from far away the neighing of the horses in Rocking-Horse Land calling to him. And in the morning with the white hair round his finger he called 'Rollonde, Rollonde!' and Rollonde neighed and came back to him, dipping and dancing over the hills.

Now this same thing happened every night; and every morning the horse kissed Freedling, saying, 'Ah! dear Prince and kind Master,' and became stock still once more.

So a year went by, till one morning Freedling woke up to find it was his sixth birthday. And as six is to five, so were the presents he received on his sixth birthday for magnificence and multitude to the presents he had received the year before. His fairy godmother had sent him a bird, a real live bird; but when he pulled its tail it became a lizard, and when he pulled the lizard's tail it became a mouse, and when he pulled the mouse's tail it became a cat. Then he did very much want to see if the cat would eat the mouse, and not being able to have them both he got rather vexed with his fairy godmother. However, he pulled the cat's tail and the cat became a dog, and when he pulled the dog's tail the dog became a goat; and so it went on till he got to a cow. And he pulled the cow's tail and it became a camel, and he pulled the camel's tail and it became an elephant, and still not being contented, he pulled the elephant's tail and it became a guinea-pig. Now a guinea-pig has no tail to pull, so it remained a guinea-pig, while Prince Freedling sat down and howled at his fairy god-mother.

But the best of all his presents was the one given to him by the King, his father. It was a most beautiful horse, for, said the King, 'You are now old enough to learn to ride.'

So Freedling was put upon the horse's back and from having ridden so long upon his rocking-horse he learned to ride perfectly in a single day, and was declared by all the courtiers to be the most perfect equestrian that was ever seen.

Now these praises and the pleasure of riding a real horse so occupied his thoughts that that night he forgot all about Rollonde, and falling fast asleep dreamed of nothing but real horses and horsemen going to battle. And so it was the next night too.

But the night after that, just as he was falling asleep, he heard someone sobbing by his bed, and a voice saying, 'Ah! dear Prince and kind Master, let me go for my heart breaks for a sight of my native land.' And there stood his poor rocking-horse Rollonde, with tears falling out of his beautiful eyes on to the white coverlet.

Then the Prince, full of shame at having forgotten his friend, sprang up and threw his arms round his neck saying, 'Be of good cheer, Rollonde, for now surely I will let thee go!' and he ran to the window and opened it for the horse to go through. 'Ah, dear Prince and kind Master!' said Rollonde. Then he lifted his head and neighed so that the whole palace shook, and swaying forward till his head almost touched the ground he sprang out into the night and away towards Rocking-Horse Land.

Then Prince Freedling, standing by the window, thoughtfully unloosed the white hair from his finger, and let it float away into the darkness, out of sight of his eye or reach of his hand.

'Good-bye, Rollonde,' he murmured softly, 'brave Rollonde, my own good Rollonde! Go and be happy in your own land, since I, your Master, was forgetting to be kind to you.' And far away he heard the neighing of horses in Rocking-Horse Land.

Many years after, when Freedling had become King in his father's stead, the fifth birthday of the Prince his son came to be celebrated; and there on the morning of the day, among all the presents that covered the floor of the chamber stood a beautiful foal rocking-horse, black, with deep-burning eyes.

No one knew how it had come there, or whose present it was, till the King himself came to look at it. And when he saw it so like the old Rollonde he had loved as a boy, he smiled, and, stroking its dark mane, said softly in its ear, 'Art thou, then, the son of Rollonde?' And the foal answered him, 'Ah, dear Prince and kind Master!' but never a word more.

Then the King took the little Prince his son, and told him the story of Rollonde as I have told it here; and at the end he went and searched in the foal's mane till he found one white hair, and, drawing it out, he wound it about the little Prince's finger, bidding him guard it well and be ever a kind master to Rollonde's son.

So here is my story of Rollonde come to a good ending.

From *Moonshine and Clover* by Laurence Housman (Jonathan Cape)
(See Note, page 145)

Zlateh the Goat

At Hanukkah time the road from the village to the town is usually covered with snow, but this year the winter had been a milder one. Hanukkah had almost come, yet little snow had fallen. The sun shone most of the time. The peasants complained that because of the dry weather there would be a poor harvest of winter grain. New grass sprouted, and the peasants sent their cattle out to pasture.

For Reuven the Furrier it was a bad year, and after long hesitation he decided to sell Zlateh the goat. She was old and gave little milk. Feyvel the town butcher had offered eight gulden for her. Such a sum would buy Hanukkah candles, potatoes and oil for pancakes, gifts for the children, and other holiday necessaries for the house. Reuven told his oldest boy Aaron to take the goat to town.

Aaron understood what taking the goat to Feyvel meant, but he had to obey his father. Leah, his mother, wiped the tears from her eyes when she heard the news. Aaron's younger sisters, Anna and Miriam, cried loudly. Aaron put on his quilted jacket and a cap with earmuffs, bound a rope around Zlateh's neck, and took along two slices of bread with cheese to eat on the road. Aaron was supposed to deliver the goat by evening, spend the night at the butcher's, and return the next day with the money.

While the family said good-bye to the goat, and Aaron placed the rope around her neck, Zlateh stood as patiently and good-naturedly as ever. She licked Reuven's hand. She shook her small white beard. Zlateh trusted human beings. She knew that they always fed her and never did her any harm.

When Aaron brought her out on the road to town, she seemed somewhat astonished. She'd never been led in that direction before. She looked back at him questioningly, as if to say, 'Where are you taking me?' But after a while she seemed to come to the conclusion that a goat shouldn't ask questions. Still, the road was different. They passed new fields, pastures, and huts with thatched roofs. Here and there a dog barked and came running after them, but Aaron chased it away with his stick.

The sun was shining when Aaron left the village. Suddenly the weather changed. A large black cloud with a bluish center appeared in the east and spread itself rapidly over the sky. A cold wind blew in with it. The crows flew low, croaking. At first it looked as if it would rain, but instead it began to hail as in summer. It was early in the day, but it became dark as dusk. After a while the hail turned to snow.

In his twelve years Aaron had seen all kinds of weather, but he had never experienced a snow like this one. It was so dense it shut out the light of the day. In a short time their path was completely covered. The wind became as cold as ice. The road to town was narrow and winding. Aaron no longer knew where he was. He could not see through the snow. The cold soon penetrated his quilted jacket.

At first Zlateh didn't seem to mind the change in weather. She too was twelve years old and knew what winter meant. But when her legs sank deeper and deeper into the snow, she began to turn her head and look at Aaron in wonderment. Her mild eyes seemed to ask, 'Why are we out in such a storm?' Aaron hoped that a peasant would come along with his cart, but no one passed by.

The snow grew thicker, falling to the ground in large, whirling flakes. Beneath it Aaron's boots touched the softness of a ploughed field. He realized that he was no longer on the road. He had gone astray. He could no longer figure out which was east or west, which way was the village, the town. The wind whistled, howled, whirled the snow about in eddies. It looked as if white imps were playing tag on the fields. A white dust rose above the ground. Zlateh stopped. She could walk no longer. Stubbornly she anchored her cleft hooves in the earth and bleated as if pleading to be taken home. Icicles hung from her white beard, and her horns were glazed with frost.

Aaron did not want to admit the danger, but he knew just the same that if they did not find shelter they would freeze to death. This was no ordinary storm. It was a mighty blizzard. The snow-fall had reached his knees. His hands were numb, and he could no longer feel his toes. He choked when he breathed. His nose felt like wood, and he rubbed it with snow. Zlateh's bleating began to sound like crying. Those humans in whom she had so much confidence had dragged her into a trap. Aaron began to pray to God for himself and for the innocent animal.

Suddenly he made out the shape of a hill. He wondered what it could be. Who had piled snow into such a huge heap? He moved toward it, dragging Zlateh after him. When he came near it, he realized that it was a large haystack which the snow had blanketed.

Aaron realized immediately that they were saved. With great effort he dug his way through the snow. He was a village boy and knew what to do. When he reached the hay, he hollowed out a nest for himself and the goat. No matter how cold it may be outside, in the hay it is always warm. And hay was food for Zlateh. The moment she smelled it she became contented and began to eat. Outside the snow continued to fall. It quickly covered the passage-way Aaron had dug. But a boy and an animal need to breathe, and there was hardly any air in their hideout. Aaron bored a kind of a window through the hay and snow and carefully kept the passage clear.

Zlateh, having eaten her fill, sat down on her hind legs and seemed to have regained her confidence in man. Aaron ate his two slices of bread and cheese, but after the difficult journey he was still hungry. He looked at Zlateh and noticed her udders were full. He lay down next to her, placing himself so that when he milked her he could squirt the milk into his mouth. It was rich and sweet. Zlateh was not accustomed to being milked that way, but she did not resist. On the contrary, she seemed eager to reward Aaron for bringing her to a shelter whose very walls, floor and ceiling were made of food.

Through the window Aaron could catch a glimpse of the chaos

outside. The wind carried before it whole drifts of snow. It was completely dark, and he did not know whether night had already come or whether it was the darkness of the storm. Thank God that in the hay it was not cold. The dried hay, grass, and field flowers exuded the warmth of the summer sun. Zlateh ate frequently; she nibbled from above, below, from the left and right. Her body gave forth an animal warmth, and Aaron cuddled up to her. He had always loved Zlateh, but now she was like a sister. He was alone, cut off from his family, and wanted to talk. He began to talk to Zlateh. 'Zlateh, what do you think about what has happened to us?' he asked.

'Maaaa,' Zlateh answered.

'If we hadn't found this stack of hay, we would both be frozen stiff by now,' Aaron said.

'Maaaa,' was the goat's reply.

'If the snow keeps on falling like this, we may have to stay here for days,' Aaron explained.

'Maaaa,' Zlateh bleated.

'What does "Maaaa" mean?' Aaron asked. 'You'd better speak up clearly.'

'Maaaa, maaaa,' Zlateh tried.

'Well, let it be "Maaaa" then,' Aaron said patiently. 'You can't speak, but I know you understand. I need you and you need me. Isn't that right?'

'Maaaa.'

Aaron became sleepy. He made a pillow out of some hay, leaned his head on it, and dozed off. Zlateh too fell asleep.

When Aaron opened his eyes, he didn't know whether it was morning or night. The snow had blocked up his window. He tried to clear it, but when he had bored through to the length of his arm, he still hadn't reached the outside. Luckily he had his stick with him and was able to break through to the open air. It was still dark outside. The snow continued to fall and the wind wailed, first with one voice and then with many. Sometimes it had the sound of devilish laughter. Zlateh too awoke, and when Aaron greeted her, she answered, 'Maaaa.' Yes, Zlateh's language

61

consisted of only one word, but it meant many things. Now she was saying, 'We must accept all that God gives us—heat, cold, hunger, satisfaction, light and darkness.'

Aaron had awakened hungry. He had eaten up his food, but Zlateh had plenty of milk.

For three days Aaron and Zlateh stayed in the haystack. Aaron had always loved Zlateh, but in these three days he loved her more and more. She fed him with her milk and helped him keep warm. She comforted him with her patience. He told her many stories, and she always cocked her ears and listened. When he patted her, she licked his hand and his face. Then she said, 'Maaaa' and he knew it meant, I love you too.

The snow fell for three days, though after the first day it was not as thick and the wind quieted down. Sometimes Aaron felt that there could never have been a summer, that the snow had always fallen, ever since he could remember. He, Aaron, never had a father or mother or sisters. He was a snow child, born of the snow, and so was Zlateh. It was so quiet in the hay that his ears rang in the stillness. Aaron and Zlateh slept all night and a good part of the day. As for Aaron's dreams, they were all about warm weather. He dreamed of green fields, trees covered with blossoms, clear brooks, and singing birds. By the third night the snow had stopped, but Aaron did not dare to find his way home in the darkness. The sky became clear and the moon shone, casting silvery nets on the snow. Aaron dug his way out and looked at the world. It was all white, quiet, dreaming dreams of heavenly splendour. The stars were large and close. The moon swam in the sky as in a sea.

On the morning of the fourth day Aaron heard the ringing of sleigh bells. The haystack was not far from the road. The peasant who drove the sleigh pointed out the way to him—not to the town and Feyvel the butcher, but home to the village. Aaron had decided in the haystack that he would never part with Zlateh.

Aaron's family and their neighbours had searched for the boy and the goat but had found no trace of them during the storm.

They feared they were lost. Aaron's mother and sisters cried for him; his father remained silent and gloomy. Suddenly one of the neighbours came running to their house with the news that Aaron and Zlateh were coming up the road.

There was great joy in the family. Aaron told them how he had found the stack of hay and how Zlateh had fed him with her milk. Aaron's sisters kissed and hugged Zlateh and gave her a special treat of chopped carrots and potato peels, which Zlateh gobbled up hungrily.

Nobody ever again thought of selling Zlateh, and now that the cold weather had finally set in, the villagers needed the services of Reuven the Furrier once more. When Hanukkah came, Aaron's mother was able to fry pancakes every evening, and Zlateh got her portion too. Even though Zlateh had her own pen, she often came to the kitchen, knocking on the door with her horns to indicate that she was ready to visit, and she was always admitted. In the evening Aaron, Miriam, and Anna played dreidel. Zlateh sat near the stove watching the children and the flickering Hanukkah candles.

Once in a while Aaron would ask her, 'Zlateh, do you remember the three days we spent together?'

And Zlateh would scratch her neck with a horn, shake her white bearded head and come out with the single sound which expressed all her thoughts, and all her love.

From *Zlateh the Goat and Other Stories*
by Isaac Bashevis Singer
(Longman Young Books)
(See Note, page 146)

The Flying Horse

There was once a young man called Bellerophon who, seeking adventure as was the custom, came to the court of the King of Lycia. There he fell in love with the King's daughter. But the King did not want him as a suitor so he said, 'If you wish to marry my daughter, you must prove your courage. Kill the Chimaera and I will give my consent.'

'The Chimaera!' cried Bellerophon in dismay, for the Chimaera was a fearsome monster which was the terror of the countryside. It had three heads, one a lion's, the second a goat's, the third a serpent's. It breathed fire and smoke so that all who came near were burnt to death.

However, Bellerophon was a brave young man. He accepted the challenge. First he went to ask the advice of a wise old man, Polydius.

'No man can come near the Chimaera and live,' said Polydius. 'You must attack the monster from the air so that you can escape quickly. Find the flying horse, Pegasus, and tame him and you may be able to vanquish the Chimaera.'

Bellerophon set out at once in search of the flying horse. He had heard that sometimes Pegasus could be found on Mount Helicon, for there was a spring of pure water there which the wonderful horse had brought from the rock with a stamp of his hoof.

Bellerophon watched and waited for a long time on Mount Helicon. One night he dreamed that the goddess Athene appeared to him and gave him a golden bridle with which to tame the wild horse. In the morning there was indeed a golden bridle beside him, for Athene wished to help him in his quest.

As Bellerophon stood, the bridle in his hand, out of the sky a beautiful silvery horse came floating down with wide spread wings and alighted on the mountain.

Bellerophon held his breath at the wonderful sight. For the moment he forgot that he must rob this beautiful creature of his freedom. He watched entranced.

Pegasus cantered to the fountain with so light and dancing a step that the grasses scarcely stirred beneath his feet. Now he ran for the joy of running, now he rolled on the ground for sheer pleasure. As he began to get to his feet again, Bellerophon darted forward and sprang on to the wild horse's back, the golden bridle in his hand.

Startled, Pegasus soared into the sky. Never before had he been ridden and he was filled with panic. He flew through the air at tremendous speed, then stopped so suddenly, his head between his legs, that Bellerophon was almost unseated. He dropped like a stone towards the earth so swiftly that the wind whistled by him, but still Bellerophon held on. At last Pegasus, mad with fury, turned his wild head and tried to bite Bellerophon. Quickly the young man slipped the bit between the horse's teeth, slid the bridle straps over his ears and clipped the gold chain.

At once Pegasus lost all his fear and anger and obeyed his master's touch. He was as gentle now as he had been wild. Without protest he carried Bellerophon to Mount Helicon again and there horse and master rested for the night.

Then began a few days in which Bellerophon and Pegasus travelled everywhere together and became friends. So much so that the young man began to think that with the help of the magical horse, he might be able to conquer the terrible Chimaera. So one morning Bellerophon buckled on his sword and shield and mounted Pegasus. Climbing steeply into the dawn sky, they flew away to find the Chimaera's hiding place in the deep valleys of Lycia. When Bellerophon saw that the land below him was laid waste and black with fire, he knew that the Chimaera must be near. Three spirals of smoke were rising from the side of a mountain. Could they be from the Chimaera's three heads?

At a touch Pegasus glided down silently and Bellerophon saw the monster in the mouth of a cave. It was even more terrible than he had imagined. Its three heads were so hideous and the fire from its nostrils so fierce that Bellerophon shuddered with dread. Summoning up all his courage, he swooped down again and as he sped past the cave he swept his sword through the air and cut off the goat's head.

Pegasus carried him safely up into the sky, ready for his next attack. This time he was not so successful for the monster was now fully alert and very angry. It sprang at him as he darted past and injured his shoulder and Pegasus' wing. But Bellerophon saw that he had at least wounded the lion's head.

On his third attack he drove straight at the monster, for this must be his last attempt. This time the Chimaera flung itself savagely on Pegasus and tried to bring him down. The magic horse climbed steeply in terror, the monster hanging on to his flanks. So great was the heat of the flames the Chimaera belched forth, that Bellerophon had to protect his face with his shield. But in the moment that the monster was off guard, the young man thrust his sword into its neck, wounding it mortally. Roaring and hissing, the Chimaera released its hold and fell to the earth. By the time it reached the ground, the fire in its body had consumed it utterly.

Wearily Bellerophon and Pegasus returned to Mount Helicon to drink of the pure water of the spring. There Bellerophon bathed Pegasus' wounds and they both rested from the terrible battle.

Now that Bellerophon had completed his task, he claimed the princess as his wife and after more tests he won her. Through all his adventures Pegasus was his faithful companion.

Alas, the two friends were parted and it was Bellerophon's fault. In his pride at his success, he boasted that he would fly to Olympus itself and challenge the gods to combat.

This could not be allowed! Zeus caused a gadfly to sting Pegasus as he flew. Startled, the horse reared so suddenly that Bellerophon fell to the earth and was killed.

But Pegasus the beautiful flying horse has never been forgotten for he became a constellation of stars that can be seen in the sky today.

Adapted by Eileen Colwell from several versions
(See Note, page 147)

Annabelle

5-7

Once upon a time there was a cow with a poorly tummy. Her name was Annabelle. And one day she saved a big ship from being wrecked.

One foggy day, on the coast of Cornwall, Annabelle was in her field eating some grass for breakfast. The fog was so thick that she couldn't see the end of her nose, and suddenly she swallowed a thistle.

Oh dear! It was in her tummy and prickled and hurt like anything. Annabelle stopped eating and mooed as loudly as she could.

Just then a big ship was sailing by on her way to America.

The Captain looked through his telescope but he could see only fog.

'Do you know where we are?' he said to his first officer.

'No, Sir! But we're somewhere off the coast of Cornwall.'

'Well, sound the hooter,' said the Captain. So the first officer sounded the hooter—'Moooo!'

Annabelle heard it, and thought, 'There's another cow who has swallowed a thistle. I must get the doctor,' and she mooed again to let the other cow know she had heard.

'Listen!' said the Captain. The first officer stopped sounding the hooter and listened. Then, from across the water, through the fog, they heard it again: 'Moo!'

'That's Annabelle Cow,' said the Captain. 'We must be near her field.' And he started giving lots of orders.

'Stip the shop!—I mean Stop the ship!'

'Reverse the engines!'

'Drop the anchor!'

'Sound the hooter!'

The ship stopped, the anchor chain rattled down and the ship's siren sounded again: 'Moooo!'

'Oh, what a poorly tummy that cow's got,' thought Annabelle, and she mooed again: 'Moooo!'

The Captain looked over the side. Soon the sun came out and the Captain saw that he had stopped the ship from hitting a rock.

He had saved the ship, all because he had heard Annabelle's moos.

Just then, he heard her mooing again: 'Mooooo! Mooooo!'

'That's funny,' he thought. 'She's still mooing, perhaps she's got a poorly tummy!' So he sent the ship's doctor ashore to make Annabelle's tummy better.

'And give her this too!' he said, and handed the doctor a little box with a big label tied to it.

When the doctor reached the shore, Annabelle was still feeling poorly but he gave her some pills and she soon began to feel all right.

'The Captain asked me to give you this,' said the doctor. He took the little box the Captain had given him and showed it to her. On the label was written:

'To Annabelle—the Cow that saved our Ship—From the Captain.'

Inside was a lovely silver medal. The doctor tied it round Annabelle's neck and the medal hung on her chest. She *was* proud.

'That's because by mooing you saved the ship. Now I must hurry back because we are going to America,' said the doctor.

He hurried to the ship. The sun shone brightly and the fog had gone.

Annabelle looked out to sea.

'Moo!' she said.

'Moo!' replied the ship.

As the ship sailed on, the moos became fainter. But the Captain, looking through his telescope, could see Annabelle eating grass with the medal round her neck.

'Moo!' said Annabelle, looking out to sea. 'Moo!'

And from the big ship, far across the water, she thought she heard a faint 'Moo!'

She was very happy and went on eating her grass, while the medal shone in the morning sunlight.

From *Time and Again Stories* by Donald Bissett (Methuen)
(See Note, page 148)

Rabbit and the Wolves

Rabbit's grandmother had given him a little pipe. Now he was skipping along through the woods, *lipperty-lipperty-lip-lip-lipperty,* and playing on his little pipe. Rabbit didn't live in the woods himself. He lived in Grandmother's house; but he had lots of friends in the woods, and his best friend of all was Marmot, who lived in a hole under a tree stump. Now Rabbit was going to show his new pipe to Marmot. He was looking forward to showing the pipe to his best friend, Marmot.

So on frisked Rabbit, *lipperty-lipperty-lip-lip-lipperty* . . . and then, oh dear, what do you think? Out from behind the trees jumped seven great wolves.

'Rabbit, we're going to eat you!'

Rabbit was a brave little fellow. If he was frightened, he wasn't going to show it. He said, 'Well, I own you've caught me fairly. But, dear me, you can't *all* eat me, you know; I'm only a mouthful. Well, which of you is it to be?'

The Wolves began to quarrel then, because they all wanted to eat Rabbit. But Rabbit said, 'Don't quarrel! Don't quarrel! I've got a good idea. Do you like dancing?'

'Of course we do! Of course we do!' cried the Wolves.

'Well then,' said Rabbit, 'I know a lovely new dance, and I was just longing to teach it to someone. Shall I teach it to you? Then the one who dances best can have me for a prize.'

The Wolves agreed that it *was* a good idea. So Rabbit said, 'This dance is in seven parts. For the first part, you get into line, one behind the other. I lean against this tree, and when I begin to sing, you all dance away from me. When I stop singing and call out *Hu!* then you dance back. But you must keep in line, and dance properly; no floundering about.'

'No, No! No floundering about!' cried the Wolves.

So Rabbit leaned against a tree and began to sing:

> 'Ha, how tasty,
> Ha, how toothsome,
> Ha, how tender,
> Little Rabbit flesh!'

And the Wolves danced away from him, keeping in line, one behind the other, and lifting their feet to the time of his singing.

'*Hu!*' cried Rabbit, when they had danced some way. And the Wolves swung round and came dancing back to him. 'Keep in line, keep in line!' cried Rabbit. 'Lift your feet neatly! Ah, that's very good . . . Yes, that was really charming!' he said, as the Wolves gathered round him.

'Now,' said he, 'we come to the second part of the dance. I go to that tree over there, and you form in line again. I sing, you dance away, and when I call *Hu*! you turn and come dancing back. This second part of the dance is very like the first, only at every fourth step you fling back your heads and give a nice little howl. Got that?'

'Yes, yes,' cried the Wolves. 'This is great fun!'

So Rabbit went and leaned against this other tree, and began to sing again:

> 'Ha, how tasty,
> Ha, how toothsome,
> Ha, how tender,
> Little Rabbit flesh!'

And the Wolves danced away, keeping in line, one behind the other, lifting their feet, and at every fourth step flinging back their heads and howling. It would have been the funniest sight in the world, if only Rabbit had felt more like laughing. But he didn't feel like laughing, you may be sure.

So, when the Wolves had danced quite a long way, he called out '*Hu!*' and the Wolves all turned and came dancing back.

'Well now, that was even better than the first time,' said Rabbit. 'In all my life I've never seen such beautiful dancing!' And he went on to a third tree. 'For this third part of the dance you do a polka,' said he. 'Do you know the polka step?'

'Of course we do!' cried the Wolves.

'Well then, off you go!' said Rabbit. And he began to sing, '*One* and *two* and *three* and *four! Hop* and *hop* and *hop* and *hop!*'

Off went the Wolves, hopping and skipping. They were laughing like anything. They were enjoying themselves so much that they had almost forgotten about eating Rabbit. Though of course Rabbit knew they would remember it again as soon as the dance ended.

'*Hu!*' he called once more, and all the Wolves came polka-ing back. 'Magnificent!' said Rabbit, moving to a fourth tree.

And what do you think cunning little Rabbit was doing, as he moved from tree to tree? Just this: with every tree he came to, he was getting nearer and nearer to the hole under the tree stump where his best friend, Marmot, lived.

So he sent the Wolves off in a fourth dance and a fifth dance, and a sixth dance, and between every dance he moved on to another tree, nearer to Marmot's hole.

'*Hu!*' he cried for the sixth time. And the Wolves came dancing back. They were really proud of themselves.

And Rabbit moved to yet another tree.

'Now this is the seventh and last part of the dance,' said he. 'It's called the Sun Dance, and it's a gallop. You go as fast as you can, and at every seventh step you turn a somersault. Understand? Well then, get ready to go. I'll count three, and then you start. But remember as soon as I shout *Hu!* you all turn round and come racing back. And then—oh dear!—the first that reaches me gobbles me up . . . Well, of course,' he added, wiping his eyes, 'one can't live for ever. But seeing you dance so beautifully has made my last moments happy . . . One, two, *three*!' he shouted, and off galloped the Wolves.

> 'Dance away, Wolves, dance away!
> See us dancing, dancing, dancing!
> We dance, we dance, we dance the Sun Dance,
> See how beautifully we dance!'

sang Rabbit.

'Dance away now, dance away!' shouted the Wolves, turning a somersault at every seventh step. 'See how beautifully we dance!'

'Hurrah!' cried Rabbit.

'*Hurrah! Hurrah! Hurrah!*' shouted the Wolves. Their voices were getting fainter and fainter. They were a long way off now. Rabbit could only just see their grey bodies flickering in and out among the trees. But something else he could see, quite close to him, and that was the tree stump where Marmot had her hole. And, bless me, if that wasn't Marmot's little anxious face, peeping out at him!

'*Hu!*' shouted Rabbit—and made a dash for the hole.

The Wolves turned and came racing back, each one determined to be first, that he might gobble up Rabbit. But what did they see when they came back to the starting place? Nothing at all!

Only from under the ground nearby they heard Rabbit singing:

> 'Dance away now, dance away,
> Dance away, Wolves, dance away!
> You won't eat Rabbit, not today,
> Not today, Wolves, not today!'

From *Tortoise Tales* by Ruth Manning-Sanders (Eyre Methuen)
(See Note, page 148)

6-9

Nella's Dancing Shoes

Once upon a time there was a beautiful Dancer called Nella. She lived in a garden in Italy. Nella was the loveliest dancer in the world, and all the people wanted her to come and dance at their parties. In the evening she would go down to Florence to their long salons hung with blue satin embroidered with flowers, or red velvet printed with gold, and dance on the polished floors under twelve enormous chandeliers glittering with lights and lustres, which hung down like long diamond ear-drops in a Queen's ears; or else she would dance in their gardens on the

74

lawns among the statues and roses and fountains, where all the trees were hung with lights like coloured stars. And whenever she danced in her rose-red velvet dancing slippers, all the people clapped their hands and shouted, '*Brava*, Nella! *Brava, brava!*'

In Nella's cupboards at home were rows and rows of other slippers, of gold, and glass, and silk, and leather; but she never wore any of them when she went to dance for the people. For the rose-red velvet slippers were magic slippers which made her dance better than anyone else in Italy; and when she wore her other slippers, she couldn't dance at all. Nobody knew this but Nella.

One day Nella was in her garden picking roses, and because the dew was on the grass she had taken off her red velvet slippers and left them by her chair. Suddenly a great Eagle swooped out of the sky, caught the slippers in his beak, and flew away as swiftly as he had come. Nella gave a scream and stood on tip-toe, and reached out her arms, trying to touch the sky. But it was no good; the slippers and the Eagle had vanished entirely.

Then Nella sat down and cried and cried. She was to dance that night for the Prince of Florence, but when the people came to fetch her she was still sitting crying in the garden, and she wouldn't tell them why. She only sobbed, and said she wouldn't dance. They entreated in vain—no! She wouldn't dance. She couldn't, of course, because she had lost her magic slippers. Every day after that she sat in the garden watching the sky, and every night the people were sad because Nella, their beautiful dancer, would dance for them no more.

One day as Nella sat watching the sky for the Eagle she saw a rush of wings overhead. It was not the Eagle, however, but a flight of Swallows.

'Oh, Swallows!' cried Nella. 'You go about in the sky as people go about on earth, so have you seen the great Eagle who stole my red velvet slippers?'

But the Swallows had never seen or heard of him, and flew away, and Nella wept.

The next day as she was watching, a flock of Wild Swans flew over her head.

'Oh, Swans!' cried Nella. 'You go over more places in a year than most men travel in a lifetime, so have you seen the great Eagle who stole my red velvet slippers?'

But the Swans could give her no news of him, and *they* flew away, and Nella wept.

The next day as she was watching, she saw a thousand Starlings twinkle like stars over her garden.

'Oh, Starlings!' cried Nella. 'You have been everywhere among the clouds, so have you in your travels ever met the great Eagle who stole my red velvet slippers?'

But the Starlings could tell her no more than the Swans and the Swallows, and they also flew away, and Nella wept.

On the fourth day as she sat in her garden a single shadow fluttered on the grass, and looking up she saw that it was made by a green Parrot with one red feather in his tail.

'Oh, Parrot!' cried Nella. 'You live in strange countries and have seen many things, so have you seen the great Eagle who stole my red velvet slippers?'

'Certainly I have,' said the Parrot.

'Oh, where?' cried Nella.

'I was sitting on a coconut-tree in a Jungle,' said the Parrot, 'and the Eagle flew over my head with your slippers in his beak. When he reached the very middle of the Jungle, he opened his beak and dropped the slippers, and that was the last I saw of him or them.'

'Oh, Parrot!' cried Nella. 'Where is the Jungle?'

'In the very middle of India,' said the Parrot, and flew away.

Then Nella began to weep again, for it seemed to her that her precious slippers might as well be in the Eagle's beak as in the middle of India, for all the use they were to her.

Just then she heard a voice say, 'Come, come, I wouldn't cry if I were you!' and looking up she saw the Fan-Man looking through the gate. He was long and thin and dressed in green, and he had a green paper fan in his hand.

'What *would* you do, then?' said Nella. 'The Eagle has dropped my red slippers in the very middle of the Jungle in the very middle of India, so there's nothing to do but cry. If I had wings like an Eagle or a Swallow or a Swan or a Starling or a Parrot, I wouldn't need to cry.'

'Tush, tush!' said the Fan-Man. 'There are more ways of flying than with wings.'

Then he came into the garden and told Nella to stand on tiptoe as though she were going to dance, and when she was on the very points of her toes he opened his fan and fanned her. Up she went into the air like a bird, and after her went the Fan-Man, fanning with all his might. He fanned her right across Italy and Turkey and Persia until they reached India; and when he had fanned her to the very middle of the Jungle, the Fan-Man stopped, and Nella dropped.

Now in the very middle of the Jungle in the very middle of India there is a Blue Pool, so Nella dropped into the Pool and went down and down and down till she got to the bottom. At the bottom of the Pool she found the Blue Nymph of the Pool sitting on a lotus leaf, and to Nella's great joy the Nymph had the red velvet slippers on. But as she had never seen slippers before, and hadn't the least idea what they were for, instead of having them on her feet she had hung them in her ears, where they dangled like a pair of red earrings.

Nella clasped her hands and cried, 'Nymph, Nymph, give me my slippers!'

'That I won't!' said the Nymph. 'They are *my* slippers, for the Eagle who brings me things brought them to me, and they are the prettiest things I ever saw.'

'Then you haven't seen those I wear on my feet,' said Nella, and she put out her little feet which happened that day to be shod in her golden slippers. They were much prettier than the red ones, though not nearly so wonderful.

But the Nymph didn't know that, and anyhow she had no use for slippers to dance in, but only to hang in her ears, so she eagerly asked, 'Will you change?'

'If you wish it,' said Nella. And she kicked off her golden slippers and put on her red ones, while the Blue Nymph hung the golden slippers in her ears, and looked more pleased with herself than before.

'Goodbye,' said Nella.

'Goodbye,' said the Blue Nymph.

Then Nella rose to the top of the Pool, where the Fan-Man was waiting for her. As soon as he saw her he spread his fan again, and in another moment she was sailing over India and Persia and Turkey and Italy. And when they came to her own rose garden, the Fan-Man stopped, and Nella dropped.

The first thing she did was to stand on her toes and dance.

The next thing she did was to send word to the town, saying, 'Tonight I will dance for the Prince of Florence.'

And that night, under thousands of stars, amongst thousands of coloured lights, Nella danced on the lawn in her red velvet slippers better than she had ever danced before, and all the people, overjoyed to have their beautiful Nella dancing for them again, climbed on the chairs and the tables, and clapped their hands, shouting:

'*Brava*, Nella! *Brava, brava!*'

From *Italian Peepshow* by Eleanor Farjeon
(Oxford University Press)
(See Note, page 149)

The Farmer's Wife and the Tiger

A story from Pakistan

One day a farmer went with his bullocks to plough his field. He had just turned the first furrow when a tiger walked up and said, 'Peace be with you, friend. How are you this fine morning?'

'The same to you, my lord, and I am pretty well, thank you,' replied the farmer, quaking with fear but thinking it wisest to be polite.

'I am glad to hear it, because Providence has sent me to eat your two bullocks,' said the tiger cheerfully. 'You are a God-fearing man, I know, so make haste and unyolk them.'

'Aren't you making a mistake, my friend?' asked the farmer. His courage had returned now that he knew the tiger was only proposing to gobble up his bullocks, not him. 'Providence sent me to plough this field and in order to plough, I must have oxen. Hadn't you better go and make further enquiries?'

'There is no need to delay, and I should be sorry to keep you waiting about,' said the tiger. 'If you'll unyolk the bullocks,

I'll be ready in a moment to eat them.' With that the tiger began to sharpen his teeth and claws in a very frightening manner.

The farmer begged and prayed that his oxen might not be eaten and promised that, if the tiger would spare them, he would give him in exchange a fine fat young milch-cow of his wife's.

To this the tiger agreed, and taking the oxen with him for safety, the farmer hurried home. Seeing him return so early from the fields, his wife, who was an energetic hard-working woman, called out, 'What! Lazy bones! Back already and my work just beginning!'

The farmer explained how he had met the tiger and that, to save the bullocks, he had promised the milch-cow in exchange. At this his wife began to shout, saying, 'A likely story indeed! What do you mean by saving your stupid old bullocks at the expense of my beautiful cow. Where will the children get milk? How can I cook without butter?'

'All very fine, wife,' retorted the farmer, 'but how can we make bread without corn? How can we have corn without bullocks to plough the fields? It's surely better to do without milk and butter than without bread, so make haste and untie the cow.'

'You great silly!' scolded his wife. 'If you had an ounce of sense in your brain, you'd think of some plan to get us out of this difficulty.'

'Think of one yourself!' cried her husband in a rage.

'So I will,' replied his wife, 'but if I do the thinking, you must do as I say. Go back to the tiger and tell him that the cow wouldn't come with you, but that your wife is bringing it.'

The farmer, who was a great coward, didn't like the idea of going back empty-handed to the tiger, but as he could not think of any other plan, he did as he was told. He found the tiger still sharpening his claws and teeth, he was so hungry. When he heard that he had to wait still longer for his dinner, he began to growl and lash his tail and curl his whiskers in a most terrible manner, causing the poor farmer's knees to knock together with terror.

Now, when the farmer had left the house, his wife went out to the stable and saddled the pony. Then she put on her husband's best clothes, tied the turban very high so as to make her look as tall as possible, jumped astride the pony and set off to the field where the tiger was.

She rode along, swaggering like a man, till she came to where the lane turned into the field, and then she called out as bold as brass, 'Now, please the powers, I may find a tiger in the field! I haven't tasted tiger since yesterday when I ate three for breakfast.'

Hearing these words and seeing the speaker ride boldly towards him, the tiger was so alarmed that he turned tail and bolted into the forest. He went at such a headlong pace that he nearly knocked down his own jackal—tigers always have a jackal of their own to clear away the bones after they have finished eating.

'My lord! My lord!' cried the jackal. 'Where are you going so fast?'

'Run! Run!' panted the tiger. 'There's the very devil of a horseman in yonder field who thinks nothing of eating three tigers for breakfast!'

At this the jackal laughed. 'My dear master,' he said, 'the sun has dazzled your eyes! That was no horseman, but only the farmer's wife dressed up as a man!'

'Are you quite sure?' asked the tiger, pausing in his flight.

'Quite sure, my lord,' said the jackal, 'and if your lordship's eyes had not been dazzled—ahem—by the sun, your lordship would have seen the woman's pigtail hanging down behind her.'

'But you may be mistaken,' persisted the cowardly tiger, 'she was the very devil of a horseman to look at!'

'Who's afraid?' replied the jackal. 'Come! Don't give up your dinner because of a woman! We'll go together, if you like.'

'No! You might take me there and then run away and leave me!' said the tiger fearfully.

'Well, let us tie our tails together then, so that I can't!' suggested the cunning jackal. He was determined not to be done out of his bones at the end of the feast.

81

To this the tiger agreed, and having tied their tails together in a reef-knot, the pair set off arm-in-arm.

Now the farmer and his wife had remained in the field, laughing over the trick they had played on the tiger. Suddenly, lo and behold, what should they see but the tiger and the jackal coming towards them with their tails tied together.

'Run!' cried the farmer. 'We are lost! We are lost!'

'Nothing of the kind, you great baby,' answered his wife coolly. 'Stop that noise! I can't hear myself speak!'

She waited until the pair of animals were within hail, then called out politely. 'How very kind of you, dear Mr Jackal, to bring me such a nice fat tiger! I shan't be a moment finishing off my share of him, and then you can have the bones.'

At these words the tiger became wild with fright, and, quite forgetting the jackal and that reef-knot in their tails, he bolted away full tilt, dragging the jackal behind him. Bumpety, bump, bump, over the stones. Scritch, scratch, scramble, through the briars!

In vain the poor jackal howled and shrieked to the tiger to stop —the noise behind him only frightened the coward more. Away he went, helter-skelter, hurry-scurry, over hill and dale, till he was nearly dead with fatigue, and the jackal was *quite* dead from bumps and bruises.

And the farmer and his wife were never troubled by the tiger again.

From *Folk Tales from Asia* retold by Ikram Chugtai
(Cultural Centre for Unesco, Tokyo)
(See Note, page 150)

Everest Climbed

The Summit

Four in a tent on the South Col, blue
And wretched, battered by wind, and frozen—
Tenzing and Hillary (the summiters Hunt had chosen)
With Lowe and Gregory there to support:
These men with Ang Nyima, and a few
On their way descending, held the fort . . .

And they churned over in thought
Each gruelling beast-of-burden week
Of carrying from base to Col and back to base
Then wearily up again, an endless chain;
Da Namgyal's blistered fingers and swollen face;
Balu crumpled, weeping like a child;
Temba stretched on the stones, with scarce a breath
In his body; and the struggle to stand and totter, with Death
One plod behind—

Oh, the freezing touch and the voices wild!—
Then, from the tired despair, one thrilling story gasped
By Evans and Bourdillon—how they'd trod
The Southern Peak and almost grasped the crown,
When trouble with snow and breathing knocked them down . . .

All day the windy peak flared
In foam-white flame, and nobody dared
To stir from where he lay.
All night, while the billowy tent bellied and reared,
They fought the cold; and the wind like a battering ram
In the frail canvas drummed and pounded—
Then at eight o'clock next day
(O miracle!) faded away.

See them crawl from the tunnelled tent,
Two men ballooned in blue and gold—
Tenzing, alert and tiger-bold;
Hillary, with the slow New Zealand drawl,
The hatchet chin
And hearty laugh and half-moon grin,
Whose legs long as the world was wide
Could take crevasse or hill at a stride.
(His was the raging mountain passion,
All guts and go and no half ration).

They checked their oxygen gauges, shouldered
Each his Atlas world of weight.
With languid gait, in sluggish tracks
Like snails with houses on their backs,
Hooped and bowed yet bright with hope
They heaved themselves up the endless slope.

High on the mountain far above
With Greg and Ang Nyima, Lowe was cutting steps.
Through a hail of icy chips

84

They cramponed into his stair and caught him up
When the sun was high overhead.
Gregory said, 'We've carried your stuff
Higher than Lhotse, far enough.'
But there was no place here to drop the gear,
No shelf for a tent. Though tired and spent,
They stumbled up the steepening ridge
Till Tenzing thought of a likely ledge
He'd seen last year in a cleft.
They traversed across and dumped their loads and left.

Here Tenzing and Hillary pitched their tent.
They scratched the snow from the frozen rock
And levelled, side by side,
Two strips of floor—two hours it took and more—
Then anchored the guys to the oxygen flasks
And panting crawled inside
The highest-smallest-coldest-frailest home
The world had known.
When Tenzing had set the primus roaring,
Soup he made from a saucepan of snow
Melted at twenty-seven below;
They spread the dainties he'd been storing—
Date and apricot, jam and honey.
As sugared lemon and ice weren't short,
They thawed and swallowed quart on quart.

The sun went down, from peak to peak
The long purple shadows creeping.
Tired and weak,
They yawned and settled down to sleeping—
Hillary bunched in his narrow place,
Tenzing stretched on the brink of space.
While the rude wind roared them a lullaby
To a tearing tune,
Hillary, sleepless, braced for each blast,

Clung to the walls and anchored them fast
And none too soon,
Till the wind sank down and the silent sky
Was lit with the stars and the moon.

At four in the morning he woke. His feet
And legs were numb to the knees and freezing.
But the peaks were aglow in the early light
And the frost was easing.
His boots were white and stiff from the weather,
So he cooked them over the primus flame
Till up to his nostrils fiercely came
The stench of burning leather.
When they'd carefully checked the oxygen gauges
And fixed their boots and loaded backs,
Away they stepped in easy stages,
Each in turn kicking the tracks.

They toiled to the foot of the Southern Peak
Where the slope was steep with snow half-stuck—
And slippery, treacherous indeed
When Hillary's turn it was to lead.
The first step firm, the second crumbled,
And down in a shower of white he tumbled.
Tenzing was ready—on the lightning slope
He halted him with axe and rope.
Thus once before in the Icefall snow
The Tiger had held him, bruised and numb,
On the icy brink of Kingdom Come
Whose chasm yawned below.

Undaunted still, with desperate skill,
Cautious as blind men crossing a street
They crept four hundred faltering feet.
And they'd reached and passed the Southern Peak
When Hillary's rope began to drag

And Tenzing staggered and fell in his track,
Tottered and swayed and gasped for breath.
The face in the icicle-crusted mask
Was pale as death.
But Hillary found where the strength was going—
The oxygen tube was jammed with ice.
With his glove he knocked it free—in a trice
The life was flowing.

Their steps were weary, keen was the wind,
Fast vanishing their oxygen fuel,
And the summit ridge was fanged and cruel—
Fanged and cruel, bitter and bare.
And now with a sickening shock
They saw before them a towering wall
Of smooth and holdless rock.
O ghastly fear—with the goal so near
To find the way was blocked!
On one side darkly the mountain dropped,
On the other two plunging miles of peak
Shot from the dizzy skyline down
In a silver streak.

'No hope of turning the bluff to the west,'
Said Hillary. 'What's that I see to the east?
A worm-wide crack between cornice and rock—
Will it hold? I can try it at least.'
He called to Tenzing, 'Draw in the slack!'
Then levered himself right into the crack
And, kicking his spikes in the frozen crust,
Wriggled up with his back.
With arms and feet and shoulders he fought,
Inch by sweating inch, then caught
At the crest and grabbed for the light of day.
There was time, as he struggled for breath, to pray
For all the might that a man could wish—

Then he heaved at the rope till over the lip
Brave Tenzing, hauled from the deep, fell flop
Like a monstrous gaping fish.

Was the summit theirs?—they puffed and panted—
No, for the ridge still upward pointed.
On they plodded, Martian-weird
With pouting mask and icicle beard
That cracked and tinkled, broke and rattled,
As on with pounding hearts they battled,
On to the summit—
Till at last the ridge began to drop.
Two swings, two whacks of Hillary's axe,
And they stood on top.

From *The Windmill Book of Ballads*
by Ian Serraillier (Heinemann Educational Books)
(See Note, page 151)

Poor Old Lady,
She Swallowed a Fly

Poor old lady, she swallowed a fly,
I don't know why she swallowed a fly,
Poor old lady, I think she'll die.

Poor old lady, she swallowed a spider.
It squirmed and wriggled and turned inside her.
She swallowed the spider to catch the fly.
I don't know why she swallowed a fly,
Poor old lady, I think she'll die.

Poor old lady, she swallowed a bird.
How absurd! She swallowed a bird.
She swallowed a bird to catch the spider.
She swallowed the spider to catch the fly.
I don't know why she swallowed a fly,
Poor old lady, I think she'll die.

Poor old lady, she swallowed a cat.
Think of that! She swallowed a cat.
She swallowed the cat to catch the bird.
She swallowed the bird to catch the spider.
She swallowed the spider to catch the fly.
I don't know why she swallowed the fly,
Poor old lady, I think she'll die.

Poor old lady, she swallowed a dog.
She went the whole hog when she swallowed a dog.
She swallowed the dog to catch the cat.
She swallowed the cat to catch the bird.
She swallowed the bird to catch the spider.
She swallowed the spider to catch the fly.
I don't know why she swallowed a fly,
Poor old lady, I think she'll die.

Poor old lady, she swallowed a cow.
I don't know how she swallowed the cow.
She swallowed the cow to catch the dog.
She swallowed the dog to catch the cat.
She swallowed the cat to catch the bird.
She swallowed the bird to catch the spider.
She swallowed the spider to catch the fly.
I don't know why she swallowed a fly,
Poor old lady, I think she'll die.

Poor old lady, she swallowed a horse.
She died, of course.

Rose Bonne
(See Note, page 152)

Room for a Little One

Bridget were the little maid at the big inn where all they travellers comes and she were on her two little feet from daybreak till the chime hours, a-running up and down with all she had to do in the kitchens, and as if that weren't enough she had to be off and gather wood from the Selwood Forest and see and bring it in for firing—great loads too— but they did think to give she a little nirrip so as she could bring two loads to the one back home. And when all t'other Christian souls was warm and snoring hours since she just about finished the washing and cleaning and mending up the fires, and then she run out shivering in her bare feet to the nirrip's stable to get warm again, crowded up against the little rough coat. 'Twas a very little nirrip and a very little stable—just a old shed with old thatch the stars shined down through, and room for a little one—but they both of they made it two and contrived to sleep sound till cockcrow.

There come one bitter cold night, snow and frost, and the inn was full up to the roof-tree, with stables and bartons full of beasts too.

Bridget and the nirrip come back numb to the bone and that loaded you couldn't see nothing under the firing but their feet, and they was like blue ice-blocks; and there in the yard were a bone-weary, clarty old hungry plough-ox, left without a mouthful of hay or shelter, and freezing to death he was, and they both couldn't have that.

'I got a stable,' says the nirrip.

'And there's be a bit of hay too,' says Bridget.

''Tis ours,' they said, 'but there's room for a little one.'

The old ox took a look at it.

One great star were a-shining down into the yard and into the stable too and somehow it did have a look big enough for a mortal freezing old ox.

91

And somehow it were.

And somehow there were quite a goodish bit of hay inside as well.

So Bridget let the nirrip creep in too—and away with her to make up the fires. She thaw her feet a bit that way and then, would you believe it, they said they'd need more wood.

Back to the girt, black forest she and the poor little nirrip must trudge again in all the bitter wind and frost, so her went to tell the creature and her nearly cried when her did. The little small thing were so stiff and numbed as she were.

"Twill be wicked black dark,' says Bridget. 'Oh, I be that a-feared to go.'

'I've a cross on my back,' says the nirrip speaking up brave.

'And that there star-a-shining above will show the way,' says the old ox comforting. 'I'll a-come back too if you do like, then us'll only be needing one girt big load.' So, tired to death as they all was, they goes to the forest.

Bridget she had a slice of stale bread from the pig bucket, and the nirrip and the old ox still chewed a bit of hay—'twasn't much but something to keep 'en from starving, and they got their load.

Then they all seed somebody under the starlight. A man and a woman 'twas, and they were just about so tired as the three of them was. The man was a-helping the woman who couldn't hardly walk no more.

'She do need shelter,' said Bridget. 'And food and a bed—and there were no room in the inn.'

'There's my stable,' said the nirrip under her great load.

'And room for a little one,' said the ox all a-shiver as he staggered.

So the man he up and took the little nirrip's wood and the woman rode on a tired, careful little back.

Ever so careful nirrip were, and they all found they was going back to inn quite fast in the starlight.

Then Bridget she saw the man and woman go thankful into the little stable, and they beckon the nirrip and the ox inside too, then they all called out to Bridget standing in the snow and star-shine all in her bare feet, 'There's room for a Little One!'

'I'll come, my dears, when I've a-done my work,' said Bridget, and away she went and dragged the wood to the hearth where the ox's master lay drink-taken and she washed and cleared up, and found a bit of clean bread and cheese.

She took that out along with her. She'd a notion they must be hungry in the stable—and the star shone bright as if it were dancing and Bridget's feet they danced too.

So out she run and the stable was all a-lit by the great star and God's dear Son was there too with the others and there was angels singing—the nirrip were a-singing too.

> 'I gave Him my manger all full of sweet hay;
> I knelt with the shepherds on Chrissimas Day.
> The Star it shone over—and loud I did bray.
> Gloria in excelsis!
> Christ the Lord is born!'

From *Forgotten Tales of the English Counties*
by Ruth Tongue (Routledge and Kegan Paul)
(See Note, page 153)

The Hero

Mother, let us imagine we are travelling, and passing through
strange and dangerous country.

You are riding in a palanquin and I am trotting by you on a
red horse.

It is evening and the sun goes down. The waste of Joradighi
lies wan and grey before us. The land is desolate and
barren.

You are frightened and thinking—'I know not where we have
come to.'

I say to you, 'Mother, do not be afraid.'

The meadow is prickly with spiky grass, and through it runs
a narrow broken path.

There are no cattle to be seen in the wide field; they have
gone to their village stalls.

It grows dark and dim on the land and sky, and we cannot
tell where we are going.

Suddenly you call me and ask me in a whisper, 'What light is
that near the bank?'

Just then there bursts out a fearful yell, and figures come
running towards us.

You sit crouched in your palanquin and repeat the names of
the gods in prayer.

The bearers, shaking in terror, hide themselves in the thorny
bush.

I shout to you, 'Don't be afraid, mother. I am here.'

With long sticks in their hands and hair all wild about their
heads, they come nearer and nearer.

94

THE HERO

I shout, 'Have a care! You villains! One step more and you
   are dead men.'
They give another terrible yell and rush forward.
You clutch my hand and say, 'Dear boy, for heaven's sake,
   keep away from them.'
I say, 'Mother, just you watch me.'

Then I spur my horse for a wild gallop, and my sword and
   buckler clash against each other.
The fight becomes so fearful, mother, that it would give you
   a cold shudder could you see it from your palanquin.
Many of them fly, and a great number are cut to pieces.
I know you are thinking, sitting all by yourself, that your boy
   must be dead by this time.
But I come to you all stained with blood, and say, 'Mother,
   the fight is over now.'
You come out and kiss me, pressing me to your heart, and
   you say to yourself,
'I don't know what I should do if I hadn't my boy to escort
   me.'
A thousand useless things happen day after day, and why
   couldn't such a thing come true by chance?
It would be like a story in a book.
My brother would say, 'Is it possible? I always thought he
   was so delicate!'
Our village people would all say in amazement, 'Was it not
   lucky that the boy was with his mother?'

From *The Crescent Moon* by Rabindranath Tagore (Macmillan)
(See Note, page 154)

High Flight

Oh, I have slipped the surly bonds of earth
And danced the skies on laughter-silvered wings;
Sunward I've climbed, and joined the tumbling mirth
Of sun-split clouds—and done a hundred things
You have not dreamed of; wheeled and soared and swung
High in the sunlit silence. Hovering there
I've chased the shouting wind along, and flung
My eager craft through footless halls of air;
Up, up the long, delirious, burning blue
I've topped the wind-swept heights with easy grace,
Where never lark nor even eagle flew;
And while, with silent lifting mind I've trod
The high untrespassed sanctity of space,
Put out my hand, and touched the face of God.

Flying Officer J. Gillespie Magee (killed in
the Battle of Britain at the age of 19)
(See Note, page 155)

The Merry-go-round

High up in the Chilterns there is a little village called Penn. The beech woods on the neighbouring hills surround it as a green and gold frame surrounds a picture. The old houses stand in a circle about the village green, eighteenth-century houses with brass knockers, and seventeenth-century houses with no knockers at all. People use their knuckles when they visit these small dwellings.

On the green there is a duck pond, where tiddlers live and water weeds grow. In the winter the children run from their homes and slide on the ice. They haven't any skates, and such things are not necessary, for they cost money. The children of Penn slide in their little strong boots, or they ride on the pond sitting in wooden boxes from the small grocer's shop which is also the post office. Some even sit on tea trays from their mothers' kitchens. They are wrapped in gay scarves and they shout till their voices ring like the church bells in the cold air.

In spring they catch each other as they race over the green and run round the trees. In summer they fish for minnows, with bent pins and pieces of string. In autumn they watch the golden leaves fly down from the trees, and they stretch out their hands to grab them. Every autumn leaf caught before it touches the earth brings good luck, as all country folk know.

Every year in September there is a Fair on the green. That is something to look forward to. The caravans and lorries laden with strange and exciting things come puffing up the long hill from the small town in the valley. Women wearing gold earrings sit at the doors of the yellow caravans, and look out at the beech woods through which they ride, keeping an eye for a rabbit or maybe a fat pheasant on the way. Men lead the piebald horses, and lurchers run behind or dart into the hedges. Motor vans

97

bring the heaviest gear, hidden away and locked up, but round the sides of the vans there are painted notices to say the horses and roundabouts are within.

Everybody is on the lookout for the Fair people, who come past the old grey church on the hill top, and sweep round the great elm tree which is a landmark, and down the road by the little stream to the village green and its houses.

At the Red House facing the green, the twins, John and Michael are the most excited of all, for they know that the Fair will be just outside their windows. They can watch it as they eat their porridge in the morning, and at night they go to sleep with the rapturous noise of the merry-go-round ringing in their ears. They hear the talk of the shows, and when a woman wearing a gold chain comes to the back door for a jug of hot water, they rush to get it for her.

The shooting ranges and the side-shows are soon set up, and the women in the caravans make fires on the green and do a little washing. They carry buckets of water from the village pond, and boil it, and wash their clothes in the open air. Then they put clothes-lines between the caravans and hang their garments up to dry. It is a busy time, and the women like to get the chance of plenty of water and no crowds.

The platform of the merry-go-round is set up, with the silvery trumpets and glass reflectors in the centre. The men lift the horses from the great van, and carry them to the gilded poles. They slip them in the sockets, and go back for more. It takes a long time to put the lovely horses in their places, and the children all stand near to watch.

One Fair day, a strange thing happened, and John and Michael still wonder if it were real or a dream. But two boys cannot have the same dream at the same time, and besides, there is the little whistle to be accounted for.

The Fair had come as usual that September day, and the boys had been out to watch the caravans arrive and to give a hand to the man at the coconut-shy, setting up the white wooden bottles— for, of course, as it was during the war, there were no coconuts.

They knew most people in the Fair, and they went to visit the old woman who was the grandmother of some of the showmen, and the great-grandmother of others. She sat at the door of her red and gold caravan, a woman incredibly old, her face dark brown, wrinkled like a wizenedy apple, her black eyes sparkling with hidden fires, her hands like claws.

'How are you, Mrs Lee?' asked John.

'Are you quite well, Mrs Lee?' asked Michael.

She turned her sharp gaze on the two boys, recognizing them at once.

'Not so good, my dears. Only middling,' said she.

'We've brought something for you, Mrs Lee,' said John.

'My mother sent it,' added Michael, and he put a little basket of cakes and honey and an egg in the old woman's hand.

'And this,' said John, dropping a rose on the top.

'Thank you, my dears. God bless you and your mother, and Good Luck be with you,' said Mrs Lee, spreading out the contents of the basket on her white apron. Then she hobbled into the caravan to put them away, and returned with something in her tight fist.

She called to them. 'Hi! My dears! Come here! I've got summat for you too. You'll always remember old Hepzibah Lee. She's got summat for you.'

Mrs Lee held out a small shining object, and John took it.

'It's a whistle,' said he. 'Oh, just what I wanted.'

'Nay, don't 'ee blow it now,' cried Mrs Lee, as he put it to his lips. 'It's summat special. It's made of bronze. I fun' it once-on-a-time, when I was burying summat in a wood. I cleaned it up. It's very old, older nor me. It's Roman they say.'

Michael and John stared at the tiny bronze whistle, which was in the shape of a dolphin, with the lips for the mouth of the whistle, and the tail at the end.

'Thank you. Thank you very much, Mrs Lee,' said Michael and he ran off with John at his side to take the basket back to the Red House, and to show the wee whistle to his mother.

They blew the little whistle, and a strange sweet note came

from it, very small, very shrill and clear as a bell. Down by the pond the horses from the Fair were being watered.

They lifted their heads and neighed in reply. The boys blew the whistle again, and there was a faint shrill whinny from somewhere else. It may have been a horse in the field behind the cottages, or a wooden horse on the merry-go-round, or even a silver horse flying in the air, invisibly galloping out of the clouds, who knows, when magic is about?

The engine puffed and the travelling-band began to move, the merry-go-round went slowly round. The people came down the road, and the Fair was open. It was dull and quiet till night, when the crowds from all the villages for miles came, but the afternoon was given up to children.

John and Michael took their pennies, and chose their favourite horses. They stood watching the merry-go-round, and two horses seemed more beautiful than the others. Their names, printed in curly letters on their necks, were Hot Fun and Spit Fire. They had scarlet saddles, and their backs were painted in green and blue and cherry-red, with diamonds of scarlet and scrolls of gold. Their mouths were open, showing white teeth and red tongues that lolled out. Their gold eyes flashed, their heads were thrown back in the speed of their running. They looked very magnificent.

The boys rode on these two all afternoon, until their money was spent. It was grand to career on these galloping horses, with their red nostrils and their carved golden manes. John stooped over his steed and patted its neck at the end of each ride, and Michael stroked the hard flank of his hobby-horse. Did they both feel a tremor in the wood, as their hands lingered there? They secretly thought so, but perhaps it was the vibration of the engine, or even the noise of the music blaring 'Daisy, Daisy, Give me your answer do,' from the bright silvery trumpets under the reflecting mirrors in the centre.

At last all the money had gone, and the two boys reluctantly went home to tea.

'I could ride for ever like that,' sighed John. 'I hope when I'm grown up I shall go on liking it.'

'Of course you will,' said his mother. 'Tonight there will be many grown-up people enjoying the horses, just like you.'

'Not quite as much,' said Michael. 'They don't really believe when they're grown up.'

They went out again in the evening to the Mystery Cave, and the Haunted House, and they spent a few more pennies there, but so many lads were coming from the farms there was no chance to get another ride on the two famous horses, Hot Fun and Spit Fire. Other people, who knew nothing of the feelings of those horses rode on their backs when the stars came in the sky and the moon looked down.

'Good night, Hot Fun. Good night, Spit Fire,' said the boys, and away they went back home to supper and to bed.

It was splendid to lie there and to listen to the music of the merry-go-round, and the Fun Fair, to hear the shouts and the laughter. They lay in their little room, listening, and talking, and then they slept.

The sounds grew quieter, the last bus went away, the last people called 'Good night,' and the showmen shut their booths and extinguished their flares.

It must have been two o'clock in the morning when Michael awoke and looked out of the window. He could see the wooden horses like ghosts, very still and pale under the moon. Here and there a glimmer of light shone from a hanging lantern. A dog barked, a horse grunted at its picket, and a splash came from the pond as something touched the water. A white owl flew over, and strange and delicious smells of foreign people, of gypsies, and horses and fair grounds came in at the window mingled with the late honeysuckle on the front of the house.

Michael could see the old gypsy woman's caravan, and a glow in the window.

'Old Mother Lee is awake too,' he thought and then he remembered the whistle. He fetched it from his trouser pocket and leaning from the window, he blew a little blast on it.

Up leapt John, pattering to his side.

'Whatever are you doing, Michael? Can you see something?' he asked.

101

'Look! Look!' cried Michael excitedly. 'Look at the horses, John.' He blew again on the bronze whistle.

Under the moon they saw that those galloping horses, fixed in their places, were moving. They were going round the circle, swinging up and down, and spinning slowly around the mirrors and silver trumpets. The engine was still, they went by themselves. There was faint music too, so soft that they could hardly hear it, but of course it might have been the wind blowing through the trees. It wasn't playing 'Daisy, Daisy, Give me your answer, do,' but something else, wild, sweet and strange.

'Come along out. Put your coat on over your pyjamas. Let's slip out and have a ride for nothing,' whispered John.

They put on their dressing-gowns and bedroom slippers, and crept downstairs to the hall. In a moment they unbolted the door and stood in the porch. Another step, and they were out on the village green.

They ran across the damp trampled grass to the merry-go-round. There was no doubt, it was moving more quickly now, swinging in its circle, with nobody riding. The horses looked like silver phantoms gliding softly through the air, up and down, as the platform revolved. The boys waited a moment, reading the names as the horses passed, and each horse moved its head and stared at them with eager eyes. Then came Spit Fire and Hot Fun. They climbed on the platform and sprang on to the horses.

'They are real,' cried John, as he felt the warm flesh under his knees, and his hands touched the smooth skin of Spit Fire's neck. Spit Fire quivered and shook its mane. The gold hair was thick and harsh, blowing in the wind.

'They are alive,' whispered Michael, and his horse, Hot Fun, turned its head and gave a faint whinny of recognition.

The horses went very quickly, they whirled round, they danced on their outstretched hoofs, they pawed the air, and neighed in high shrill tones. They swung and reared and bucked and the boys clung to the reins, not knowing whether to be rather frightened or to be filled with exhilaration and joy. After their first surprise they enjoyed it more than anything they had ever known.

Then Michael blew his whistle, just a little blow at it, in the excitement. The cool high note flew out under the moon, and the horses all tossed their heads and whinnied back. Down from the platform they leapt, down on to the village green, and the boys held tightly to their horses' necks, lest they should be thrown.

'Goodness, Hot Fun! Where are you going?' asked John.

'Spit Fire, what's the matter?' cried Michael.

The horses galloped across the grass, between the caravans and past the booths to the duck pond. They all dipped their heads and drank the water. Six and thirty little horses were there, encircling the pond. How deeply they drank! They were very thirsty, for they had not tasted water for a long time.

Then one horse swung round and galloped across the green, and another followed, till all of them were off. They went along the road, and their little hooves made such a clatter one would think that everybody would have been wakened by them. Their stiff gold manes shone in the moonlight, their bright eyes glistened as the horses looked sideways and shied at the moon-shadows.

Gallop! Gallop! Gallop! they went, and then they sobered down and began to trot.

Trot! Trot! Trot! they went all along the white road.

Michael and John were breathless with the excitement of that night ride. They held their reins tightly, and kicked with their heels and pressed the horses' sides with their knees. Their old dressing-gowns floated behind them like wings, their hair was on end, but although they might have been cold, they felt the warmth of their steeds under them, and the beating of hearts.

Gallop! Gallop! went the horses again, and they careered past the old grey church, with its lych-gate on the top of the hill. The ancient tomb stones were criss-crossed with moonlight, and the yew trees were dead black. Past the school they went, round by the Crown Inn, with its roses and ivy on its mullions, and down to the valley and the woods.

There, under the beech trees, they stopped, and the boys got off. The horses pushed their way into a field, and began to eat the sweet grass.

'It's Farmer Pennington's field,' said Michael.

'There's his mare, watching us,' said John.

The white mare was staring at this company of six-and-thirty little horses. She shook her head and whinnied loudly, and they all replied in their own language. She came slowly across, and nuzzled them with her nose. The boys sat on a gate and watched her. She had a word with every one of those little horses, but what she said I cannot tell. It was a secret among them all.

Then Michael blew his little whistle, and what a commotion there was! The little horses came cantering three abreast, and the two boys only just managed to catch the reins and leap up on the backs of Spit Fire and Hot Fun before they went out to the road.

Away they went, back to the Fair. The moon had gone, the fields and the churchyard were misty in the milk-white air of dawn. The corncrake was calling in the barley field, and the yaffle flew over. The little horses scampered down the road to the green. They leapt up to the empty platform, and climbed to their places.

John and Michael clambered down, and patted their horses' necks. The horses were breathing quickly, and steam rose from them.

'I hope they won't get cold,' said John. 'We ought to rub them down, really.'

They stood near for a few minutes, and even as they waited the horses were turned back to wood, their wild life was calmed, and they stayed stiffly in their places, with no breath or motion.

'Good night, Spit Fire. Good night, Hot Fun,' called the boys. Then they tucked up their dressing-gowns and ran back to the house. The door was ajar as they had left it. They went upstairs to bed, tossing their soaking slippers on the carpet, throwing their damp dressing-gowns on the floor.

'Give one more blow at the whistle,' said John, as they looked through the window at the Fair.

Michael put his hand in the dressing-gown pocket. The whistle had gone!

'It must have fallen out when we sat on the gate,' said he, sadly.

'No, you had it after that,' said John. 'You must have lost it when we got off the horses, at the end. We will look for it tomorrow.'

The merry-go-round stood still, the silver horses were dusky in the mist. A light was shining in Mrs Lee's caravan.

'She's been waiting for the horses to come back,' said John.

'I expect she knew all about it,' agreed Michael.

They were very sleepy the next day, and their mother was puzzled over their damp slippers and some rents in their dressing-gowns. Briars and burrs were stuck to the wool, and silver horsehairs were on their pyjamas.

'Oh, we had a great adventure!' they cried. 'We went riding in the middle of the night.'

'Riding?' echoed their mother. 'In the night?'

'Riding on the roundabout horses, mother. We went off to Farmer Pennington's field, and the horses drank from the pond, and ate the grass.'

'Which horses? You've been dreaming, my dears.'

'The little hobby-horses, of course. When we blew the whistle, mother. But we lost it.'

'Then go and look for it, John and Michael,' said their mother. 'It was a beautiful whistle.'

They hunted high and low, but they couldn't find it. All day the merry-go-round whirled, and the horses cantered in their circle, but there was no little whistle to set them free. The boys rode on Spit Fire and Hot Fun, but there was no beating heart, or answering whinny.

Early the next day the Fair went away. The vans were loaded, the merry-go-round was packed, and the great engines puffed and snorted and dragged them along the road, across the green, past the pond, and far away.

Then Michael saw something shining in the grass. He stooped and picked up the little bronze whistle.

Quickly he blew it. From far up the road came an answering call. All the little horses, packed in the van, whinnied back in shrill tiny cries of recognition, and the piebald ponies and horses of flesh and blood drawing the caravans also whinnied.

Old Mrs Lee was sitting at the door of her red and gold caravan at the end of the procession looking over the bottom door. She waved her brown hand to the little boys.

'I see you've been a-blowing yon whistle,' she called.

'Thank you! Yes, Mrs Lee!' they replied.

'Good Luck and God bless you,' she cried, as the caravan lurched away.

'God bless you, too,' called the boys, and that was the last they saw of her.

The Fair comes every year, and they blow the whistle, but Mrs Lee is no longer in her caravan, and the little wooden horses never leave their places in the ring. However, some day, some day, who knows what may happen?

From *John Barleycorn* by Alison Uttley (Faber & Faber)
(See Note, page 155)

The Hare and the Baboons

One day Hare met Baboons on the road.

'Good day to you, Hare.'

'Good day, Baboons.'

'Hare, where are you going?'

'Baboons, I am searching for water.'

'The water is far, Hare, for the rivers are dry.'

'Yes, Baboons, it is far; I search for a water-hole and the sun is hot.'

'Come with us, Hare.'

'Why should I come with you, Baboons?'

'Because, Hare, we go to drink beer at a certain place. And it is because of this beer which we shall drink that we are happy.'

'I will come with you, Baboons, because I am very thirsty and very tired. And it is because of my thirst that I am sad.'

So Hare and Baboons journeyed together joyfully.

And when they came to a certain place where the beer was,

Baboons climbed up into the top of a high tree, for the beer-pot was in a high tree.

And Baboons said, 'Where is that fellow Hare who said he was so thirsty?'

And Baboons called, 'Come up, Hare; come up, Hare; come up to the beer-drink.'

But Hare could not go up because a hare cannot climb a tree.

And Baboons laughed very much because of the trick which they had played with Hare.

And Baboons began to drink the beer.

And Hare was very angry with Baboons because of the trick, and because the day was very hot, and because of his thirst, and because he was very tired.

And Baboons kept on drinking the beer and laughed very much. But Hare went home, thinking how he might do some hurt to Baboons because of the trick.

And when he had made his plan, Hare went out to search for Baboons, and he found them.

'Good day to you, Baboons.'

'Good day to you, Hare.'

'Baboons, will you drink beer with me?'

'Yes, Hare, we will drink with you gladly. When shall we come, Hare?'

'Tomorrow you must come, Baboons; tomorrow at midday, when the sun is very hot. You must come to the open space.'

And Baboons agreed. And Baboons laughed very much because of the beer which they would drink.

And Hare also laughed because he was a very cunning fellow.

But next day, early in the morning, Hare took some fire to the open space and burned all the long grass there. But in the middle of the space Hare saved a small patch. And in the small patch of unburnt grass Hare put the beer-pot.

And at midday, when the sun was very hot, Baboons came running to the small patch of unburnt grass in the open space. And they found Hare there.

And Baboons were very tired because the sun was hot, and

they were tired because of their running.

'Good day to you, Hare.'

'Good day to you, Baboons.'

'Is the beer ready, Hare?'

'Yes, Baboons, it is ready.'

'Then let us drink, Hare, for we are very thirsty.'

'Yes, Baboons, we will drink, but the beer-pot is a new pot; it is one borrowed from a friend. I have promised my friend that his pot shall not be made dirty by unwashed hands. Therefore we must first see that our hands are clean, and after that we may take hold of the pot and drink the beer.'

And when Baboons looked at their hands, they saw that they were very black, because they had run over the burnt grass to the small patch in the open space.

And Hare said, 'Baboons, you must go to the water and wash your hands, and when they are clean you can come back to the small patch, and after that we will drink the beer.'

And Baboons ran off.

And after they had washed their hands at the water, they returned and said, 'Hare, we are ready, let us now drink the beer.'

And Hare said, 'Yes, but I must first see that your hands are clean because of the pot.'

And when Hare saw Baboons' hands he was very angry, and said, 'Baboons, how is this, did you not agree to wash your hands because the beer-pot is a new pot?'

Now Baboons' hands were as black as before because they had again run over the burnt grass of the open space to the small patch.

And again Hare said, 'Baboons, you must go back to the water and wash your hands, and when they are clean you shall come back to the small patch, and after that we will drink the beer.'

And again Baboons ran off to the water to wash, and again they came back. And many times they went and many times returned; but always, when they came back, their hands were as black as before because of the burnt grass of the open space.

And when at sunset Baboons returned no more, Hare saw that

they were too tired with much coming and going. And Hare laughed very much and said, 'Who is it who can make a fool of the Cunning One?'

And Hare took up the pot of beer and carried it to his home, and he and his wife and his children drank the beer.

From *African Aesop* by Frank Worthington (Collins)
(See Note, page 156)

I went to the Animal Fair

I went to the animal fair,
The birds and the beasts were there,
By the light of the moon
The giddy baboon
Was combing his auburn hair.
The monkey gave a jump
Right on to the elephant's trunk,
The elephant sneezed
And fell on his knees
So what became of the monkey, monkey,
monkey, monkey monk . . .

(Now you start all over again and
continue as long as you have breath.)

(See Note, page 157)

The Signalman

'Halloa! Below there!'

When he heard a voice thus calling him, he was standing at the door of his signal-box with a flag in his hand, furled round its short pole. One would have thought that he could not have doubted from what quarter the voice came; but instead of looking up to where I stood at the top of the steep cutting, he turned and looked down the Line. There was something remarkable about his manner of doing so.

He raised his eyes and saw my figure high above him.

Just then there came a vague vibration in the earth and air, quickly changing into a violent pulsation and an oncoming rush that caused me to start back as though it had force to draw me down. When the vapour from this rapid train had passed me, I looked down again and saw him refurling the flag he had shown while the train went by.

'Is there any path by which I can come down?' I called.

He seemed to regard me with fixed attention, then with a singular air of reluctance or compulsion, he pointed out the path. The cutting was extremely deep and precipitous. It was made through clammy stone that became wetter as I descended the zigzag path.

When I came down low enough, I saw that he was standing between the rails. He was a dark and sallow man with a dark beard and heavy eyebrows. His attitude was one of such expectation and watchfulness that I stopped for a moment, wondering at it.

His post was in as solitary and dismal a place as I ever saw. On either side a dripping-wet wall of jagged stone, like a great dungeon, excluding all view but a narrow strip of sky; ahead a gloomy red light and the gloomier entrance to a black tunnel. So little sunlight ever found its way to this spot, that it had an earthy, deadly smell; and so much cold wind rushed through it, that it struck chill to me as if I had left the natural world.

'This was a lonesome spot to occupy,' I said, 'and a visitor was a rarity, I should suppose. Not an unwelcome rarity, I hoped.' There was something in the man that daunted me.

He directed a most curious look towards the red light and looked all about it as if something were missing from it, and then looked at me. The monstrous thought came to me as I looked at his fixed eyes and saturnine face, that this was a spirit, not a man.

'You look at me,' I said, forcing a smile, 'as if you had a dread of me.'

'I was doubtful,' he returned, 'whether I had seen you before — *there*,' and he looked towards the red light.

'I never was there,' I replied. 'Why should I be?'

His manner cleared and he replied to my questions about his work. Yes, he had long and lonely hours, but he had grown used to it.

He took me to his box where there was a fire, a desk for an official book in which he had to make entries, a telegraphic instrument and an electric bell. He was several times interrupted by the little bell and had to read off messages and send replies. While he was speaking to me he twice broke off with a fallen colour, turned his face towards the little bell when it did *not* ring, opened the door of the hut and looked out towards the red light near the mouth of the tunnel. Each time he came back with a strange expression which I could not interpret. 'Is there anything the matter?' I asked.

'I am troubled, sir, I am troubled,' he said. 'It is very difficult to speak of. If ever you make me another visit, I will try to tell you.'

I offered to come down again the next night and he seemed pleased. As I went he said in his low voice, 'I'll show my white light till you have found the way up. When you have found it, do not call out! What made you call "Halloa! Below there!" tonight?'

'Heaven knows! For no particular reason.'

'You had no feeling that those words were sent to you in any supernatural way?'

'No,' I replied in surprise. It seemed to me that the place struck colder.

He wished me goodnight and held up his light.

The next night at eleven he was waiting for me with his white light. We walked side by side to the signal-box and closed the door. As soon as we were seated, he began in a tone little above a whisper. 'I took you for someone else last evening.'

'Who?'

'I don't know. I never saw the face. The left arm is always across the face and the right arm is violently waved—this way.'

I followed his action with my eyes. It was that of an arm gesticulating with the utmost passion and vehemence. 'For God's sake, clear the way!' The words came into my mind unasked.

'One moonlight night,' said the signalman, 'I was sitting here when I heard a voice cry, "Halloa! Below there!" I started up, looked from that door and saw this Someone else standing by the red light near the tunnel, waving as I just now showed you. The voice cried, "Look out! Look out!" and then again, "Look out! Halloa! Below there!" I caught up my lamp, turned it to red and ran towards the figure, calling, "What's wrong? What has happened?" It stood just outside the entrance to the tunnel. I advanced so close to it that I wondered at its keeping the sleeve across its eyes. I ran right up to it and had my hand stretched out to pull the sleeve away—there was no one there. It had vanished.

'I ran on into the tunnel. I stopped and held my lantern above my head . . . Nothing. I looked round the red light, went back to my box and telegraphed both ways, "An alarm has been given. Is anything wrong?" The answer came back both ways, "All well."

'Within six hours of the Appearance, the accident on this line happened, and within ten hours the dead and the wounded were brought along the tunnel over the spot where the figure had stood.'

A disagreeable shudder crept over me. He took my arm and glanced over his shoulder with hollow eyes. The wind and the wires took up the story with a long lamenting wail.

He resumed. 'A week ago the spectre came back. Ever since it has been there by fits and starts.'

'What does it do?'

He repeated if possible with increased passion and vehemence, that former gesture that I had put words to, 'For God's sake, clear the way!'

Then he went on. 'I have no peace or rest for it. It calls to me for many minutes together, "Below there! Look out! Look out!" It rings my bell—'

'Did it ring your bell yesterday evening while I was here?'

'Twice.'

'My eyes were on the bell and my ears were open to the bell, and it did *not* ring at those times.'

He shook his head. 'The ghost's ring is a strange vibration in the bell. *I* heard it.'

'And did the spectre seem to be there when you looked out?'

'It *was* there—both times. What troubles me so dreadfully is the question: What is the spectre trying to tell me? Where is the danger? Some dreadful calamity will happen. What can I do? No one will believe me if I telegraph "Danger". They would think I was mad. I am only a signalman. Why does the spectre not appear to somebody with power to act?'

He wiped his hands and his forehead. His state of mind was pitiable to see. I stayed with him until two in the morning, then left, promising to come again and try to reassure him. I knew not what I ought to do, but I hesitated to inform anyone of his state of mind without his permission.

Next evening the sun was not yet down when I came to the deep and gloomy cutting. I stepped to the brink and mechanically looked down from the point from which I had first seen him. I cannot describe the dread that seized me when, close to the mouth of the tunnel, I saw the appearance of a man with his left sleeve across his eyes, passionately waving his right arm.

In a moment I saw that this appearance of a man was a man indeed, not a spirit, and that there was a little group of other men standing at a short distance, to whom he seemed to be rehearsing the gesture he made. Against the tunnel a little hut, no longer than a bed, had been erected.

With a horrified sense that something was wrong, I descended the path with all the speed I could make.

'What has happened?' I asked the men.

'Signalman killed, sir.'

'*Not* the man belonging to his box?'

'Yes, sir. His body's in there, sir,' pointing to the small hut.

'How did it happen?' I asked, sick at heart.

'He was cut down by an engine, sir. It was just at broad day. He had struck the light and had the lamp in his hand. As the engine came out of the tunnel, his back was towards her . . . Show the gentleman, Tom.'

The man, the engine driver, stepped back to his former place at the mouth of the tunnel.

'Coming round the curve in the tunnel, sir,' he said, 'I saw him at the end like as if I saw through a telescope. There was no time to check speed and I knew him to be very careful. As he didn't seem to take heed of the whistle, I shut it off when we were running down upon him and shouted to him as loud as I could.'

'What did you say?'

'I said, "Below there! Look out! Look out! For God's sake, clear the way!"'

I felt a thrill of horror. 'And then?'

'I never left off calling him. I put my arm before my eyes not to see and I waved this arm to the last—but it was no use. He just stood there . . .'

It was the signalman's own death that the spectre had foretold.

Adapted and abridged from *The Signalman* by Charles Dickens
(See Note, page 157)

Two of Everything

Mr and Mrs Hak-Tak were rather old and rather poor. They had a small house in a village among the mountains and a tiny patch of green land on the mountain side. Here they grew the vegetables which were all they had to live on, and when it was a good season and they did not need to eat up everything as soon as it was grown, Mr Hak-Tak took what they could spare in a basket to the next village which was a little larger than theirs and sold it for as much as he could get and bought some oil for their lamp, and fresh seeds, and every now and then, but not often, a piece of cotton stuff to make new coats and trousers for himself and his wife. You can imagine they did not often get the chance to eat meat.

118

Now, one day it happened that when Mr Hak-Tak was digging in his precious patch, he unearthed a big brass pot. He thought it strange that it should have been there for so long without his having come across it before, and he was disappointed to find that it was empty; still, he thought they would find some use for it, so when he was ready to go back to the house in the evening he decided to take it with him. It was very big and heavy, and in his struggle to get his arms round it and raise it to a good position for carrying, his purse, which he always took with him in his belt, fell to the ground, and, to be quite sure he had it safe, he put it inside the pot and so staggered home with his load.

As soon as he got into the house Mrs Hak-Tak hurried from the inner room to meet him.

'My dear husband,' she said, 'whatever have you got there?'

'For a cooking-pot it is too big; for a bath a little too small,' said Mr Hak-Tak. 'I found it buried in our vegetable patch and so far it has been useful in carrying my purse home for me.'

'Alas,' said Mrs Hak-Tak, 'something smaller would have done as well to hold any money we have or are likely to have,' and she stooped over the pot and looked into its dark inside.

As she stooped, her hairpin—for poor Mrs Hak-Tak had only one hairpin for all her hair and it was made of carved bone— fell into the pot. She put in her hand to get it out again, and then she gave a loud cry which brought her husband running to her side.

'What is it?' he asked. 'Is there a viper in the pot?'

'Oh, my dear husband,' she cried, 'what can be the meaning of this? I put my hand into the pot to fetch out my hairpin and your purse, and look, I have brought out two hairpins and two purses, both exactly alike.'

'Open the purse. Open both purses,' said Mr Hak-Tak. 'One of them will certainly be empty.'

But not a bit of it. The new purse contained exactly the same number of coins as the old one—for that matter, no one could have said which was the new and which the old—and it meant, of course, that the Hak-Taks had exactly twice as much money in the evening as they had had in the morning.

'And two hairpins instead of one!' cried Mrs Hak-Tak, forgetting in her excitement to do up her hair which was streaming over her shoulders. 'There is something quite unusual about this pot.'

'Let us put in the sack of lentils and see what happens,' said Mr Hak-Tak, also becoming excited.

They heaved in the bag of lentils and when they pulled it out again—it was so big it almost filled the pot—they saw another bag of exactly the same size waiting to be pulled out in its turn. So now they had two bags of lentils instead of one.

'Put in the blanket,' said Mr Hak-Tak. 'We need another blanket for the cold weather.' And, sure enough, when the blanket came out, there lay another behind it.

'Put my wadded coat in,' said Mr Hak-Tak, 'and then when the cold weather comes there will be one for you as well as for me. Let us put in everything we have in turn. What a pity we have no meat or tobacco, for it seems that the pot cannot make anything without a pattern.'

Then Mrs Hak-Tak, who was a woman of great intelligence, said 'My dear husband, let us put the purse in again and again and again. If we take two purses out each time we put one in, we shall have enough money by tomorrow evening to buy everything we lack.'

'I am afraid we may lose it this time,' said Mr Hak-Tak, but in the end he agreed, and they dropped in the purse and pulled out two, then they added the new money to the old and dropped it in again and pulled out the larger amount twice over. After a while the floor was covered with old leather purses and they decided just to throw the money in by itself. It worked quite as well and saved trouble; every time, twice as much money came out as went in, and every time they added the new coins to the old and threw them all in together. It took some hours to tire of this game, but at last Mrs Hak-Tak said, 'My dear husband, there is no need for us to work so hard. We shall see to it that the pot does not run away, and we can always make more money as we want it. Let us tie up what we have.'

It made a huge bundle in the extra blanket and the Hak-Taks lay and looked at it for a long time before they slept, and talked of all the things they would buy and the improvements they would make in the cottage.

The next morning they rose early and Mr Hak-Tak filled a wallet with money from the bundle and set off for the big village to buy more things in one morning than he had bought in a whole fifty years.

Mrs Hak-Tak saw him off and then she tidied up the cottage and put the rice on to boil and had another look at the bundle of money, and made herself a whole set of new hairpins from the pot, and about twenty candles instead of the one which was all they had possessed up to now. After that she slept for a while, having been up so late the night before, but just before the time when her husband should be back, she awoke and went over to the pot. She dropped in a cabbage leaf to make sure it was still working properly, and when she took two leaves out she sat down on the floor and put her arms round it.

'I do not know how you came to us, my dear pot,' she said, 'but you are the best friend we ever had.'

Then she knelt up to look inside it, and at that moment her husband came to the door, and, turning quickly to see all the wonderful things he had bought, she overbalanced and fell into the pot.

Mr Hak-Tak put down his bundles and ran across and caught her by the ankles and pulled her out, but, Oh mercy, no sooner had he set her carefully on the floor than he saw the kicking legs of another Mrs Hak-Tak in the pot! What was he to do? Well he could not leave her there so he caught her ankles and pulled, and another Mrs Hak-Tak so exactly like the first that no one would have told one from the other, stood beside them.

'Here's an extraordinary thing,' said Mr Hak-Tak, looking helplessly from one to the other.

121

'I will not have a second Mrs Hak-Tak in the house!' screamed the old Mrs Hak-Tak.

All was confusion. The old Mrs Hak-Tak shouted and wrung her hands and wept, Mr Hak-Tak was scarcely calmer, and the new Mrs Hak-Tak sat down on the floor as if she knew no more than they did what was to happen next.

'One wife is all *I* want,' said Mr Hak-Tak, 'but how could I have left her in the pot?'

'Put her back in it again!' cried Mrs Hak-Tak.

'What? And draw out two more?' said her husband. 'If two wives are too many for me, what should I do with three? No! No!' He stepped back quickly as if he was stepping away from the three wives and, missing his footing, lo and behold, he fell into the pot!

Both Mrs Hak-Taks ran and each caught an ankle and pulled him out and set him on the floor, and there, Oh mercy, was another pair of kicking legs in the pot! Again each caught hold of an ankle and pulled, and soon another Mr Hak-Tak, so exactly like the first that no one could have told one from the other, stood beside them.

Now the old Mr Hak-Tak liked the idea of his double no more than Mrs Hak-Tak had liked the idea of hers. He stormed and raged and scolded his wife for pulling him out of the pot, while the new Mr Hak-Tak sat down the floor beside the new Mrs Hak-Tak and looked as if, like her, he did not know what was going to happen next.

Then the old Mrs Hak-Tak had a very good idea. 'Listen, my dear husband,' she said, 'now, do stop scolding and listen, for it is really a good thing that there is a new one of you as well as a new one of me. It means that you and I can go on in our usual way, and these new people, who are ourselves and yet not ourselves, can set up house together next door to us.'

And that is what they did. The old Hak-Taks built themselves a fine new house with money from the pot, and they built one just like it next door for the new couple, and they lived together in the greatest friendliness, because as Mrs Hak-Tak said, 'The new Mrs Hak-Tak is really more than a sister to me, and the new Mr Hak-Tak is really more than a brother to you.'

The neighbours were very much surprised, both at the sudden wealth of the Hak-Taks and at the new couple who resembled them so strongly that they must, they thought, be very close relations of whom they had never heard before. They said: 'It looks as if the Hak-Taks, when they so unexpectedly became rich, decided to have two of everything, even of themselves, in order to enjoy their money more.'

From *The Treasure of Li-Po* by Alice Ritchie (Hogarth Press)
(See Note, page 159)

The Good Little Christmas Tree

One snowy Christmas Eve a peasant father walked home through the forest carrying a little Christmas Tree for his children.

It was neither a very tall nor a very fine tree; while the peasant, being a poor man, had no money to deck it about with gold and silver tinsel, dolls, kites, toys, and all the rest, but he did not worry overmuch about it. He knew his wife would discover something in the chest to make the little tree look splendid, and his children, who had never had such a thing in the house before, would be very well pleased.

When he reached home, having tied up the little Christmas Tree in a sack, he bundled it into a corner of the kitchen behind the stove, and nothing that his boy and girl could say or do could persuade him to say a word about it.

They danced about his legs, pointing, peering, and asking a thousand curious questions, while the father only shook his head; but if they approached too close to the stove to have a better look at the mysterious bundle he shouted out: 'Take care! Take care! There is a wolf in the sack!' till they ran to hide themselves behind their mother with little shrieks of terror and excitement.

Presently they grew tired of teasing and went to bed; and when the father and mother were sure that both slept soundly they took the Christmas Tree out of the corner, and set it in a pot, where the mother hung among its branches a number of little brown cookies that she had baked, tied with a scarlet thread out of the chest.

The little tree looked very proud and fine, and at first the peasant and his wife admired it with all their hearts, but little by little doubt crept in, for like all parents they wished the best for their little children, and in five minutes they were sighing and

124

shaking their heads like two pine-trees on a hill as they said to each other:

'What a pity we have not the smallest silver star nor thread of tinsel to make the branches glitter!'

'How fine a few bright candles would look among the bushy needles! How the children's eyes would sparkle to watch them flicker!'

'How dingy the branches seem! So green and bare! If we had but a few small toys and gifts for our little ones, how they would clap their hands and jump for joy!'

'However, they are good, unselfish children,' the parents agreed, preparing to go to bed; 'they will think the tree very pretty as it is, and make the best of it.'

So off they went, sighing a little, and leaving the little Christmas Tree alone on the kitchen floor.

The tree sighed too, when the peasant and his wife were gone to bed, for they were an honest pair, and he liked their kind and simple hearts. The children, too, were well brought-up and cheerful, deserving the best that could come to them. If he could have crowded his humble branches with stars, diamonds, toys, bright ornaments, and playthings, the little Christmas Tree would have done so in a moment to please so worthy a family, and he stood there for a long while thinking deeply, with the cookies on their scarlet threads dangling from his branches like so many little brown mice.

All at once the little tree quivered. One by one he gently pulled his roots out of the pot. He moved so carefully that not a speck of earth fell upon the clean kitchen floor as he moved across to the door and peeped outside.

The snow lay white and deep all around. The pine-trees drooped with it, but the world was well awake. Far up in the Heavenly Meadows the baby Angels were preparing for a party.

There were wolves prowling in the forest, and a pedlar, resting for the night, burned a bright fire to keep them away.

Mass was being sung in the far-off church, while by the light of the moon gnomes and goblins were digging for diamonds under the snow.

125

Down by the stream a poor boy fished through a hole in the ice, hoping to get something for his supper, and Old Father Christmas, whom the peasants sometimes call St Nicholas, came walking through the forest with a sack over his shoulder.

The little Christmas Tree closed the door quietly behind him, running out into the snow with the cookies on his branches bobbing up and down like little brown mice as he hurried along.

He ran into a clearing where the gnomes and goblins were digging for diamonds. So busy were they that scarcely one looked up to notice him.

'What will you take for a few of your diamonds?' the little Christmas Tree asked the nearest goblins.

'Ten green needles! Ten green needles!' said the goblins, who used Christmas-tree needles for threading their necklaces of precious stones.

But when the little Christmas Tree handed over his needles and had received three diamonds in exchange, the goblins suddenly caught sight of the cookies hanging on his branches, and called out:

'Ten green needles and a round brown cookie!'

Now the little Christmas Tree did not intend to part with any of the cookies the peasant mother had made for her children, but in order to pacify the goblins he had to give them first another ten, and then a further dozen, of his green needles, after which he left them and trotted on his way, with the diamonds sparkling among his branches and the cookies bobbing up and down like little brown mice.

When he had left the goblins far behind he came on a circle of scarlet toadstools, so bright and splendid with their red tops all spotted with white that he knew it would delight the children to see a few peeping from among his needles.

But he had hardly helped himself to a handful before he heard a terrible baying, which came nearer and nearer and nearer. Surrounding him was a ring of wolves, their tongues hanging out, their eyes green and hungry.

'Don't you know better than to pick scarlet toadstools?' they asked the little Christmas Tree. 'Don't you know that every time you pluck one a bell rings in the Wolves' Den?'

'What will you take for your red toadstools?' the little Christmas Tree asked, trembling with fear.

'Twenty green needles! Twenty green needles!' said the wolves, who used Christmas-tree needles for picking thorns out of their paws. But when the little Christmas Tree had plucked the needles they noticed the cookies hanging among his branches, and growled out:

'Twenty green needles and two brown cookies!'

Now the little Christmas Tree did not intend to let the wolves have any of the cookies the mother had baked for her children, so he made one bound out of the circle, shaking a shower of sharp needles into the wolves' faces, sending them howling into the forest. He then went on his way, with the toadstools gleaming, the diamonds glittering, and the cookies bobbing about like little brown mice.

Now he came to a stream out of which all movement seemed frozen. But underneath the ice the fish still swam in the current, and here, beside a bridge hung with silver icicles, a poor boy had made a hole in the ice and was fishing for his supper.

The Christmas Tree was about to cross the bridge when he noticed the icicles, and thought how pretty a few would look hanging from the tips of his boughs like spears.

'What will you take for a few of those icicles?' he asked the fisher-boy.

'They are not mine to sell,' the poor boy replied. 'God made the icicles; I suppose He means us to take what we please. But pray tread carefully, or you will frighten away my little fishes.'

The little Christmas Tree was so pleased with the boy's courtesy that when he had broken away a few beautiful icicles he handed some of his own green needles to the fisher-boy to make new hooks.

The boy thanked him gratefully, but his eyes strayed so wistfully towards the cookies hanging among the branches that the little tree felt much perplexed. He could not part with any of the cookies the peasant mother had made for her children, but said: 'If you wish, you may take one bite out of my largest cookie, for I feel sure that is what any mother would wish!'

The boy did eagerly as he was told, and immediately felt as if he had risen from a banquet of roast goose, turkey, venison, plum pudding, mince-pies, jellies and dessert, while the little Christmas Tree hurried on his way, with the icicles sparkling, the toadstools gleaming, the diamonds glittering, and the cookies bobbing about like little brown mice.

Soon he met a procession of people who were wending their way through the forest to church.

All were carrying candles which they lit as they passed through the door, where already a great number of people were singing and praising God.

The little Christmas Tree crept in behind them to listen. In the nave stood trees a great deal taller than he, their branches ablaze with coloured candles that flickered as if they too were singing anthems.

The little tree dared not ask for a candle, so he stood close by the door, listening and watching for quite a long while.

Presently an old man and a young girl came into the church. The girl took coloured candles out of her basket, lighted them, and tied them on to the branches of the little Christmas Tree.

'There! That will please the good angels and amuse some poor child on Christmas morning,' said the girl.

But the old man grumbled:

'Look at all those cookies hanging on the branches! They will do no good there! They will go bad! The mice will eat them during the night! They ought to be cut off and given to the poor!'

The little Christmas Tree trembled so much at the old man's words that quite a shower of green needles fell on the floor round the young girl's feet, and, as she and the old man walked up the church to join the singing, the little tree quickly slipped through the door and out into the forest, with the candles flickering, the icicles sparkling, the toadstools gleaming, the diamonds glitter- ing, and the cookies bobbing about like little brown mice.

Soon he had left the church far behind. Deep in the forest he came upon a pedlar sitting by his dying fire. Beside him all his wares were spread out on the snow—puppets, boats, knives, ribbons, shawls, a fine wooden horse and a dainty little pair of red slippers.

'What will you take for that wooden horse, and that dainty pair of slippers?' asked the little Christmas Tree.

'Enough wood to make my fire blaze. I am freezing to death!' replied the pedlar.

The little Christmas Tree began to throw handfuls of his green needles into the fire, but they only smouldered. Then he broke off some of his lower twigs. They crackled a little and went out. Then he broke off his best branch, and the fire burst into a bright blaze.

The pedlar gave the wooden horse to the little Christmas Tree, but when he saw the cookies hanging on the branches a greedy look came into his eyes and he said:

'If you want the slippers too, you must give me three of those round brown cookies!'

But the little Christmas Tree did not intend to part with any of the cookies the peasant mother had made for her children.

'Oh no!' said he, 'that was not in our bargain at all! But I will give you another branch to keep your fire alight, and you shall give me the red slippers.'

The pedlar grumbled and complained, but before he could change his mind the little Christmas Tree threw another branch on the fire, picked up the slippers, and ran away with them into the forest, with the wooden horse prancing, the candles flickering, the icicles sparkling, the toadstools gleaming, the diamonds glittering, and the cookies bobbing about like little brown mice.

He ran right into the Heavenly Meadows where the baby Angels were holding their party. They were so pleased to see him they clustered round him, caressing him with their soft little wings. Their pink toes peeped out from under their white nightgowns, and they clapped their little pink hands together in joy and delight.

129

When they had danced around him nearly a hundred times they began to tie their brightest stars to his boughs. No wonder that the little Christmas Tree glowed with pleasure and gratitude!

He had very few needles left on his branches, but he offered them all as playthings to the baby Angels.

But when they grew tired of playing with the pretty green needles they began to beg for the cookies, stretching out their little hands for them and clamouring, as children will.

Now the little Christmas Tree did not intend to part with any of the cookies the peasant mother had made for her children, but the baby Angels had been so kind to him, and their rosy faces were so beseeching, that he had not the heart to refuse them, so at last he said: 'Each of you may take a tiny bite out of just one cookie, for I feel sure that is what any mother would wish!'

But when the baby Angels had had one bite they all wanted another, and to escape them the little Christmas Tree had to take to his heels and run until he had left the Heavenly Meadows far behind, with the stars shining, the slippers flapping, the wooden horse prancing, the candles flickering, the icicles sparkling, the toadstools gleaming, the diamonds glittering, and the cookies bobbing about like little brown mice.

He ran till the forest was dark again, and there he found a pool, so deep and so clear that the ice had not covered it at all.

'I will have just one drink of cool water,' said the little Christmas Tree. 'Then I must be going home.'

But when he bent over the pool and saw his reflection in the moonlight he was so overcome by his miserable appearance that he shrank back into the snow as if he wished to hide himself completely.

Gone were his bushy needles with their pale green tips, the jaunty fingers outstretched from each sturdy bough. Some of the boughs themselves were gone, leaving jagged, miserable stumps behind.

It was as if the stars, the slippers, the horse, the candles, the icicles, the toadstools, and the diamonds hung on the arms of some ragged scarecrow!

He was ashamed to go home!

While the little Christmas Tree lay almost dying of shame in the snow, someone came tramping through the forest, bringing with him joy and gladness.

St Nicholas is the children's saint. Sometimes they call him Old Father Christmas, and sometimes Santa Claus, and they credit him with all kinds of strange tricks and ways. They say he drives reindeer across the starry skies, halting them on snowy roofs to dive down chimneys with loads of gifts for stockings, sabots, and shoes. They leave presents for him, milk and cake and wine, and hay in the shoes for his reindeer. They know very little about him, but they say a great deal, and every little child loves him dearly.

Tonight the saint carried a splendid Christmas Tree over his shoulder, nearly as tall as a house, and every branch with needles.

When the little Christmas Tree saw him coming through the trees he rose up trembling with shame, huddling his poor bare branches round him as if to make himself out to be as small as a little berry bush close by.

'Oh please, kind sir,' said the little Christmas Tree. 'Please grant me a favour, for pity's sake!'

When St Nicholas stopped to listen to him the little tree began very fast and piteously: 'I beg you, kind sir, to take off my branches the shining stars, the slippers, the wooden horse, the icicles, the toadstools, the diamonds, and, above all, the little cookies tied with scarlet thread, and to tie them on the branches of that splendid tree you carry! Then of your kindness will you take the tree to the cottage at the end of the forest, and leave it at the door? For I have become such a scarecrow,' said the little tree, sobbing, 'that I am ashamed to go home!'

But St Nicholas smiled very kindly at the little Christmas Tree, stroking him with his hand on his poor, bare branches.

At the first touch the tree prickled all over! At the second he had the strangest sensation, as if each twig were bursting and popping open like so many buttons!

His needles were growing again!

As they grew thicker and thicker, new boughs sprang from the torn stumps till, reflected in the forest pool, he now saw a splendid tree, among whose branches shone bright stars and dangled silver icicles.

The candles, slippers, horse, toadstools, diamonds, and cookies were almost hidden behind the wealth of fresh green that covered the tree from top to toe.

'We will go home together!' said Old Father Christmas.

As they walked through the quiet forest they passed the Heavenly Meadows, and all the baby Angels fell in procession behind them. The pedlar left his glowing fire and followed behind the Angels. The people were leaving church. They joined the pedlar, still singing their Christmas hymns. The boy at the frozen stream picked up his basket of silver fish to follow the crowd, while the wolves skulked out of the trees, mild as lambs, trotting with the rest.

The gnomes and the goblins put down their picks and shovels to follow the wolves, while in front of them all walked St Nicholas and the little Christmas Tree, with the stars twinkling, the slippers dancing, the wooden horse galloping, the candles flaming, the icicles dazzling, the toadstools shining, the diamonds flashing, and the cookies bobbing about like little brown mice, each with a tiny bite taken out of it, except the largest, which had two!

The peasant's children were awake and peeping through the window, as children will on Christmas night.

'Look! Look what is coming through the forest! Look at the wolves! Look at the gnomes and goblins! Look at the sweet little Angels in their white nightgowns! Look at the people singing, and the poor boy carrying his basket of fish! Look at the pedlarman! and *look*! . . . there is Old Father Christmas, and he is bringing us a little Christmas Tree all covered with . . . Oh! quick! quick! get back into bed and pull the bedclothes over our heads as quick as we can, or we shall never get anything at all!'

The Good Little Christmas Tree by Ursula Moray Williams (Hamish Hamilton) (See Note, page 159)

FOR THE STORYTELLER

For the Storyteller

I have selected the particular stories in this collection because I know that they have pleased children of various ages, and because I liked them before ever I told them. No one can tell a story successfully if he or she is not in sympathy with it. Having chosen a story the next step is to absorb it—although not necessarily to learn it by heart—until it becomes part of you. Only then shall we respond instinctively to its moods and action in pace, tone and gesture. We are only a vehicle, an interpreter, it is the *story* that matters.

In most cases I have not attempted to give detailed suggestions as to how to tell the story—everyone has their own natural way of storytelling—but I have tried to bring out the significant aspects or points which need to be emphasized.

The suggestions I have made as to audience age appeal are approximate only. Children vary so in powers of comprehension and appreciation—and in concentration also—that it is impossible to be rigid about age grouping.

The telling-time is also approximate. It all depends on one's way of telling a story and the conditions under which it is told. Other factors may also cause it to move more quickly or more slowly.

I have included only two poems of the many which might have been chosen. Response to poetry relies on individual taste, but *some* boys will appreciate the ecstasy and poignancy of *High Flight* and *some* girls will be entranced by the sound and feeling of *A Girl Calling*. Poetry can be introduced into storytime in a natural way and as an extension of our own pleasure in it. Who knows what it may mean to some child as an imaginative experience?

The participation rhymes are for shared fun and to relieve

tension when the audience has been silent and still for a long while. But it is wise to consider your environment. If, for instance, you are in a library, perhaps next to the reference library, adults may not be altogether sympathetic to a loud cheerful noise from the children! It is dangerous to use these rhymes if one cannot control an audience.

A storytelling notebook is helpful to remind us of the stories we would like to tell again. Note particulars of the source of the story, its telling time and the kind of audience to which it may appeal. Jot down the opening and closing sentences and make a brief outline of the plot and action. These details are an invaluable aid to memory when the story is to be told again.

John Masefield said in his autobiography, *So Long To Learn*, 'If the story be worth the knowing, it is worth the sharing; it can only become a story when shared.' How many good stories still await that sharing!

EILEEN COLWELL

Notes for the Storyteller
The Magic Umbrella

Telling time: 7 minutes.
Audience: Children of 6 upwards and adults.

The Magic Umbrella is a good example of how a story can develop through audience participation. On looking at the original story after many years—it has been out-of-print for some time—I find that it has acquired a new ending and additional characterization. It has a simple pattern and is very human. Its humour is slap-stick. It invites participation in the counting for the spell and I usually ask the children to whistle so that the spell will be sure to work. This is only advisable, by the way, if you are able to control your audience!

This is the kind of story in which everyone knows what is going to happen from the beginning but enjoys it all the more for this pleasurable anticipation. When the counting of seven is reached, pause a second, then, without a word, look upwards at the imaginary church steeple and every child will know that it has happened at last—the old lady is circling round the church steeple, the magic umbrella in her hand.

Characterization is obvious, although it need only be suggested by small details. Imagine the farmer's wife, a simple homely soul much bewildered by the strange things that are happening to her, and her not-very-bright daughters. I have suggested a dialect, Lancashire or Yorkshire, but it can be from wherever seems suitable. In London and the south of England, the use of the Lancashire 'Ee-ee' appears to be irresistibly funny; in Lancashire it would seem part of everyday language and could be replaced by some other dialect word.

In Rose Fyleman's original the climax I have described in detail was only suggested as a possibility. But I found that children waited for the story to take the old lady up the steeple, so I began to invent the expected ending. Now this has settled into the form I have used here and it seems to satisfy the audience. After disposing of the old lady's malady, say BUT and pause before adding the last sentence, 'If you should find an umbrella . . ' (This final sentence was in the original story).

137

The Magic Umbrella is a simple story with a fairy tale pattern of magic which is set in such an everyday environment that it seems completely credible. The beginning of the story must be told slowly enough for every child to absorb what will happen when the storyteller counts three, five or seven.

This has, I think, been the most generally popular story of any I have told. I have shared it with children of all ages and audiences at home and abroad, in multi-racial Canada and North America, in Germany and Holland, and they have been able to understand it. It must be remembered, however, that when telling stories to those whose first language is not English, it is essential to *speak clearly* and not too fast.

Fierce Feathers

Telling time: 15–20 minutes.
Audience: Boys and girls of 9 upwards.
Occasion: For use in a church or Sunday School, as well as in libraries and schools.

I came across this story some years ago—it was written about 1916— and I was impressed by it. Here was a story about American Indians, but from what a different angle! It was a story of danger and courage, a story which could suggest new ways of looking at life. Above all it was *true*. All storytellers know the child who says accusingly, 'But did it really happen?' *Fierce Feathers* was true and memorable and teachers have told me of its continued impact on modern children.

The setting is a Quaker Meeting-house in North America in the eighteenth century. The social and political background can be suggested in such detail as is suitable for the age of the children listening to the story.

Slow down your story a little as the visiting Friend speaks the text which is the keynote of the tale. It is from the ninety-first Psalm and the words of the Authorized Version must be used, for the more modern translations are not as vivid nor as apt. 'He shall cover thee with His feathers and under His wings shalt thou trust.' This needs no simplification, but it might be as well to repeat these words again, for it is likely that many modern children will not be familiar with them.

As the Meeting sinks into its customary silence, the sleepy comments of the two children alert the audience as to what is to happen. Most children will soon realize the significance of the 'feathers' and will wait in suspense for the Indians to appear.

The wordless battle between the Quaker leader and the Indian Chief must not be hurried or glossed over, for this is as important as any battle in the field. It is the victory of love over hatred and violence which results in the surrender of the Indians to stillness and peace.

The rest of the story should be told at a good pace for it is almost an anti-climax; indeed, I am tempted to summarize the friendly meal and the conversation. However, the story needs to be rounded off by the repetition of the text from the psalm as a final reminder of the story's meaning.

I have cut the story slightly for there have been many versions, and I have omitted one or two sentences which might be considered derogatory to the Indians.

A good story, worth telling well, *Fierce Feathers* needs to be studied and absorbed so that the storyteller is truly in the spirit of the story. For some children it will be a memorable experience.

Molly Whuppie

Telling time: 12 minutes.
Audience: Boys and girls of 8 upwards.

Molly Whuppie is a well-known traditional tale with several fairy tale themes woven into it—parents abandon their children because they cannot bear to see them starve, a giant plans to kill the lost children but attacks his own children in error, three treasures are stolen from the giant. All these themes are retained but because Walter de la Mare has rewritten the story, there are subtle differences which give it warmth and make it more visual. Above all the character of Molly is more developed than in the original, rather bald, narrative. De la Mare has made her a real person, brave, resourceful, gay and almost cheeky, her sisters' champion and truly feminine.

Note the touches of description which complement the text—the King's palace stands beside a pool 'full of wild swans'; each of Molly's three visits to the giant's house is different in detail for she dresses differently and hides in a different place. Her exploits are made plausible. Compassion is here too. Molly's father sends his children into the forest with bread and treacle to stay their hunger; the giant is not allowed to kill his children but locks them up in the cellar; the giant's wife (who is treated rather unkindly) presumably escapes death.

The collection from which this story is taken is an interesting one. In *Tales Told Again*, De la Mare presents well-known tales but touched by a poet's imagination and by the compassion of a sensitive and gentle man. It is not always desirable to retell traditional tales, but a new presentation in such hands as these can add to the pleasure and interest of the story.

Tell this story briskly and with gaiety. It is not a tragic tale. Concentrate on Molly for she dominates the story. One can imagine her rather enjoying the danger most of the time and 'cocking a snook' at the clumsy giant as she skips across the Bridge of the One Hair. Make the most of the three episodes in which Molly steals the giant's treasures. Imagine her waiting in hiding, her heart beating with fear and excitement. Then come her breathtaking thefts followed by the triumphant but fearful race to cross the narrow swaying bridge.

The last sentence is to me the very essence of Walter de la Mare. There are lights in all the windows, 'lights so bright that all the dark long the hosts of the wild swans swept circling in space under the stars . . .'

The Death of Balder

Telling time: 12 minutes.
Audience: Boys and girls of 10 upwards.

The Norse myths are often neglected as story material, yet they have a wealth of interest and drama and can inspire admiration for heroism and loyalty. A cycle of storytelling could well be built round these stories, from the origin of the gods to their last battle. This particular story is, I think, a suitable introduction to Norse mythology for it has captured the imagination of many young people. C. S. Lewis said that when he heard the lines:

> 'I heard a voice that cried,
> Balder the beautiful
> Is dead, is dead—'

140

he was instantly uplifted 'into huge regions of northern sky'.

There are many retellings of the story and I have built my own after reading several of them. For storytelling, this has meant some simplification.

Throughout the story there is alternation of hope and despair, joy and sadness, light and shadow. The story begins in this way with the contrast between Balder the Sun-god and Hodur his brother, blind and gloomy in his darkness. There is a strong feeling of foreboding all through the story, for Odin knows what must follow Balder's death. Mark the changes of mood in the pace of your story, the happiness of the gods as they sport against Balder, the sudden grief and horror as he is killed; the return of the triumphant messengers sure that everyone weeps for Balder, and Thökk's defiance which spells ruin to their hopes.

The characters are clearly defined—Balder himself and Hodur his opposite; Frigga and Odin, and as a foil to them all, the essentially evil Loki, the personification of malice, hatred and envy. Your voice will suggest these varying characters in some degree—it could not help but do so if you have really absorbed the feeling of the story and its tragedy.

Not a cheerful tale perhaps, but one that could well be memorable. Older boys and girls might well appreciate it, for they do not always want only the superficial and they like to be touched emotionally, to be made to *feel*. They cannot but be aware of the evil and tragedy in their own world. Such a story as this has something to say to them.

A Woman sat by the Churchyard Door

Audience: Boys and girls of about 10.

This will recall memories to some adults of sing-songs round the camp fire, and, ideally, this is where it should be used, for darkness and firelight provide the most apt setting.

The narrator recites the lines, working up the atmosphere, and the children wail the ghostly chorus. They are usually so intent upon this, their part in the proceedings, that when the climax comes they are quite unprepared for the blood-curdling scream the narrator produces.

This is not really suitable for use with a large audience—it would be too shattering—but with a small group of not-too-young boys and girls. Most children enjoy the creepy feelings induced by ghost stories and in this case there is comfort for the nervous in the company of a group.

The Elephant's Picnic

Telling time: 5 minutes.
Audience: 6 upwards.

A nonsense story which is useful to satisfy a demand for 'another story' when time is short. The fun depends upon the literal interpretation the elephant and the kangaroo give to the child's description of a picnic. If a kettle is to be boiled for tea, you put it in a saucepan and boil it, of course. What else would you do with it? If you have a trunk, you pack it with all you need. Children wear pyjamas when they go to bed, so the kangaroo, who has no pyjamas, cannot go to bed. There is a queer kind of logic in this absurd situation.

Give the children time to imagine the nonsensical happenings in the story and tell it with a twinkle in your eye as you share the fun. The child will be thinking—as you did when you first read the story—that a kettle will not become tender however long it is boiled. The ridiculous surprise ending is all the more enjoyable when it comes. For a second the children feel uncertain—you can't really eat a kettle can you?—then comes the laughter.

Brief as the story is, the elephant and the kangaroo emerge as different characters. The elephant is 'very silly', but the kangaroo is even sillier.

If you are the kind of adult who secretly thinks stories of this kind are stupid, don't tell this one. It needs the kind of acceptance a child gives it—'It's silly but it's fun!'

The Woman of the Sea

Telling time: 8–10 minutes.
Audience: 10 upwards and adults.

The seal woman who marries a human being but returns to her own people when she discovers her lost sealskin is a familiar theme in folklore. This story should be told quietly for it has pathos and ends in tragedy for the human beings in the story. From the first moment it evokes a dream-like atmosphere as we catch a glimpse of the strange sea-people dancing on the deserted beach in the moonlight. Although the fairy woman is a good wife to the young man, she is never quite of his world. One imagines her to be quiet and gentle, lulled into acceptance by her love for her children.

Keep to the phrasing of the story, for every word counts in this brief tale. Short as it is, it is rich in images—the fairy people who cast no shadow, the young man setting his bride down before the glowing fire in the dark cottage, and the fairy woman floating on the surface of the sea with the great seal at her side.

The climax of the story is the moment when the woman, her lost seal-skin in her hand, turns to go indoors again to her human life and the wind brings the sound of the sea to her. This is the pause between her two lives. Don't hurry it, but when her decision is made, quicken your pace as she hurries down to the sea, deaf even to the voices of the children she loves.

Try to convey the urgency and fear of the husband as he runs down to the shore and his despair as he sees the wife he loves already lost to him and hears her voice 'like the sound of the sea' for the last time. Use the phrase from the beginning of the story to bring it full circle. 'Then she dived to the fairy places at the bottom of the sea . . . where there comes neither snow nor darkness of night and the waves are as warm as a river in summer'. The ending must be final and brief.

Care should be taken not to tell this story to too young an audience, for the idea that a mother can leave her loved children for ever may affect some sensitive and imaginative children too strongly. This is the kind of story that older girls might appreciate and adults certainly do.

A Girl Calling

Audience: Girls of 10 upwards.

Why not make it the custom to introduce a poem during a storytelling time? This can be done naturally and unobtrusively by choosing one which is in tune with the story which has just been told. Obviously the field of choice is infinite and must be left to the storyteller's own judgement and taste.

143

The poem I have included, Eleanor Farjeon's *A Girl Calling*, is only one of the many that might be introduced in this way. It would follow quite naturally after one of the more romantic fairy tales such as *The Sleeping Beauty*, (especially in Walter de la Mare's version). It has the same feeling of magic, a dream-like quality and a felicitous use of words and rhythm which enchants the ear as well as the imagination.

Learn it just as it is written, following its form on the page and the punctuation. This is how the poet meant it to be said.

Stan Bolovan

Telling time: 12–15 minutes.
Audience: Children of 8–11.

First published in 1902 in Andrew Lang's *Violet Fairy Book*, this is a story from the Slavic but has variants in Iceland and the Smoky Mountains of North America. Stan Bolovan and his wife are unhappy because they have no children. Stan consults a wise man and on returning home finds that he now has *one hundred* children. Not unnaturally this creates problems and Stan only earns enough money to support his over-large family by outwitting a dragon.

The story begins rather slowly and children are apt to lose interest, so it is advisable to summarize the opening pages and simply say that Stan and his wife want to have children but have none. From this point there is action enough to hold the audience and Stan's various encounters with the dragon and his mother provide humour and suspense.

Stan Bolovan is a real character study—resourceful and quick-witted, naturally afraid at times but overcoming his fear in spite of the odds against him. The dragon is stupid and cowardly and his mother is not at all a nice old lady! The climax is effective and funny. The thought of one hundred children rushing forwards with knives and forks at the ready, is enough to scare any dragon. This is a good dramatic situation and a funny one. It is followed only by a brief paragraph and this is right. Anything else would be an anticlimax.

This is not a difficult story to tell or to memorize. It is straightforward and leads on from one encounter to another, each more daring than the last. The story holds the children's attention because they are curious to know how Stan will get out of such awkward situations. A slight pause before each solution will add to the pleasure of anticipation. Otherwise tell the story at a good pace—it is fun!

Rocking-Horse Land

Telling time: 15–20 minutes.
Audience: Children of 9 upwards.

Although the hero of this story is only five—it is as well not to emphasize this—the story is suitable for much older children because of its length and the way in which it is written. Prince Freedling has too many birthday presents and is bored with them all except for the magnificent rocking-horse, Rollonde. At night Rollonde comes to life and Freedling allows him to go home to his own land. Each morning he must return, for Freedling has the power to call him back. But Freedling learns that if you neglect the thing you love, you are not worthy of it, so he gives his well-loved Rollonde his freedom.

Children can understand such a fantasy as this mainly because it is based on familiar ground: home, birthdays, toys. A little abridging is allowable; for instance, in the long descriptions of the two presents given to Freedling by his fairy godmother and Prince Freedling's 'duty' letter to his godmother. I feel strongly too that the story should end when Prince Freedling unwinds the white hair from his finger and gives Rollonde his freedom for ever. The added episode of the meeting of Freedling's son and Rollonde's foal, seems sentimental and anti-climactic. Laurence Housman's style is at times a little pedantic but this can be easily amended if the storyteller feels it to be really necessary.

Keep in mind as you are telling the story the typical movement of a rocking-horse, up and down, to and fro, 'its feet motionless behind and before'. Throughout the story there is a feeling of rhythmic movement. Because it is always in the night and moonlight that Freedling and Rollonde have the power to speak to each other, there is a dreamlike atmosphere about these parts of the story. So quiet is the sleeping palace at these times, that the storyteller must perforce speak more softly for fear of breaking the spell. In the daytime the tempo of the telling is swifter, for then Freedling is a boy who is full of energy and leads his knights to battle as he rides on Rollonde's back.

145

A pleasant story, one of the handful most suitable for children amongst Housman's many fairy tale fantasies.

Zlateh the Goat

Telling time: 15 minutes.
Audience: Children of 8 upwards.

Isaac Bashevis Singer is of Eastern Europe and Jewish origin. His stories are of life amongst Jewish families and can be macabre, but this is a simple tale of human affection for a pet animal. Zlateh is a goat who must be sold to the butcher because the Jewish household is so poor. On the way to town, a blizzard forces Aaron to take refuge with Zlateh in a haystack. But for Zlateh, Aaron could not have survived the three days they are imprisoned.

The theme is one children can well understand and have sympathy with. There is no question of showing character by voices here, for Aaron and his goat are the only speakers and Zlateh's response is limited to 'Maaaa'. However this one sound can be used with different cadences to suggest Zlateh's undoubted understanding of his friend Aaron's conversation! It seems fitting also that this expressive sound should be the final word of the story.

The story is written by a craftsman with words. There are felicitous phrases which the storyteller can enjoy. It must be told with the sympathy the author feels for simple people to whom affection and the basic values of life are all-important.

I find it as well to omit one phrase in the interests of storytelling. Aaron finds the haystack and the text says, 'Aaron realized immediately that they were saved.' This destroys the hearer's suspense for, at that moment in the story, he does not know that Aaron and Zlateh will be saved. The events which make this certain are yet to come.

Since using this story I have been told that a film has been made of it. No doubt it is enjoyable but no child *needs* the help of a film to see the goat, the boy and the snowy scene. It is all there in the child's imagination, called forth by the words the author uses so skilfully.

The Flying Horse

Telling time: About 6 minutes.
Audience: Boys and girls of 8 upwards.

It is sad that many modern children are not familiar with the Greek myths. If only for their allusions which have become part of our language, it would be desirable that children should know them, but there are more important reasons than this. For older boys and girls particularly, they have much to say.

One of my favourites has always been the story of Pegasus and I have found that children like it too. The concept of a beautiful horse not bound to the earth but free to fly above the clouds, is an appealing one. That horse and man should together defeat a terrible monster that could not be slain by man alone, gives satisfaction. Hawthorne's versions of the Greek myths are out of fashion today, but the story of Pegasus while sentimental and prosy in parts, does recognize the wonder and beauty of the wild horse and Bellerophon's reluctance to tame it. Most other retellings dismiss this aspect as unimportant. Surely some imagination is legitimate in such a story and some emotion too. So I have kept this feeling for the relationship between horse and man in my retelling and built up the story from several versions otherwise. Because this is a story for younger children, some of the adult complications, as for instance the queen's desire for Bellerophon and her anger when he refuses her advances, have been omitted. I have concentrated on the story of Bellerophon and Pegasus and the slaying of the Chimaera, for this is what is of most interest to children.

This will be a straightforward piece of storytelling, of courage and the comradeship between man and beast, and it needs no other directions than the story suggests. The names are kept to a minimum—the only necessary ones are those of the hero, the horse and the monster. Children often find it very confusing to hear strange and unfamiliar names—a pity that Bellerophon's name is not simpler. I shudder to think how children would spell it! It is unnecessary to give the King and Queen a name. Neither does it add anything to relate Bellerophon's other trials of strength in order to win the princess. There are conflicting accounts of these in any case.

There are many other Greek myths which might be told, notably *The Golden Touch, Ceres and Persephone.* A good collection to consult is Roger Lancelyn Green's *Old Greek Fairy Tales.*

Annabelle

Telling time: 4–5 minutes.
Audience: Children of 5–7.

It is always refreshing to find material that is sheer nonsense and Donald Bisset's stories are just this. In this particular tale, the simple nature of the heroine and her ailment add to the fun. All children have experienced the discomfort of 'a poorly tummy'.

In just over five hundred words Annabelle is taken ill, a big ship is saved from disaster, Annabelle is cured and earns a shiny medal. Incongruity is part of Donald Bisset's secret of success. No time is wasted on descriptive passages or the building up of character, but tragedy strikes at once. Annabelle swallows a thistle and 'Oh dear! It was in her tummy and prickled and hurt like anything!'

A story like this must be told in a 'dead pan' way and with every sympathy for Annabelle's sufferings. Murmurs of concern come from the youngest children, snorts of laughter from the older ones. Obviously the story must be told as it is written—there are no superfluous words—and it is easy to memorize.

Annabelle can inspire children to produce their own illustrations of ships and strange-looking cows and impressive medals. It is a useful story for odd moments, and a valuable addition to a storyteller's repertoire.

Rabbit and the Wolves

Telling time: 7 minutes.
Audience: Boys and girls of 6–8.

A folk tale from the Appalachian Mountain Indians. This version is from a little-known collection by Ruth Manning-Sanders.

Rabbit is very like the traditional Brer Rabbit in his cunning and wit. Small as he is he outwits seven large and stupid Wolves in an entertaining and ingenious way. The idea of a dance in seven parts is intriguing and Rabbit's ironic comments about the Wolves' dancing add to the fun— 'Charming! . . . Delightful! . . . Never in my life have I seen such beautiful dancing!' Even young children know that such remarks are not sincere.

It is essential to bring out the fact that Rabbit is moving to another tree at every part of the dance, so that the children will understand his plan when it is explained. Don't forget to say at the beginning of the story that Rabbit has a friend who lives in the wood under a hollow tree stump. The audience may not know what a marmot is but in this case it doesn't really matter.

Rabbit's 'song' should be chanted or sung, to a guitar if you like. The Wolves must dance to the rhythm of the song and if necessary the words can be a little differently phrased in order to accentuate the rhythm. 'Away danced the Wolves—keeping in line—one behind the other—lifting up their feet—in time to the song,' or something like this. At every new part of the dance, the new movement can be added. After all, it is probable that the story was danced and sung originally. It should be told briskly with each new dance a surprise, especially the polka. (Surely the polka goes, 'One, two, three, *hop*,' not, 'One and two and three. Hop and hop and hop?')

Be as pathetic as you like when Rabbit reminds the Wolves that he is their prize and will be eaten. As the Wolves bound away, turning somersaults, the pace of your telling gets quicker and quicker, until even Rabbit is carried away and shouts 'Hurrah!' But when the Wolves race back to their starting point, what do they see— NOTHING!

Then comes Rabbit's mocking song from his refuge underground. This is certainly the end of the story but for very young children it may be wise to say reassuringly, 'But, of course, the Wolves never did catch Rabbit. He was much too clever for them!'

Nella's Dancing Shoes

Telling time: 8 minutes.
Audience: Children of 6–9, especially girls.

This story originated as what Eleanor Farjeon called a 'Choosing Story'. Each child chooses something—in this case a pair of red dancing slippers, an eagle, a jungle and a fan—and these must be woven into a story immediately. The more incongruous the items, the better. With an imagination as fertile as Eleanor Farjeon's, a story was created at once and as she was staying in Italy at the time, the background became Florence.

Eleanor Farjeon loved fantasy but she also had a great deal of common sense, so early in the story she states firmly that Nella's wonderful dancing is due only to the magic shoes she wears, 'without them she cannot dance at all.' This must be made quite clear to the children or the whole point of the story is lost.

There are three characters only, Nella the dancer, the Fan-Man and the Nymph of the Blue Pool. The Fan-Man is matter-of-fact although he has magic powers. 'There are more ways of flying than with wings,' he states and fans Nella halfway round the world without fuss. I can only think of Nella and the Blue Nymph as children, the one rather vain and given to childish despair, the other a spoilt and rather silly child. The brief conversation between these two is typical of exchanges between children. That the Nymph should not know the proper way to wear shoes is considered the height of humour by young children.

Note the alliteration and repetition. Swallows, Swans and Starlings fly over Nella's garden. Of each Nella asks the same question, 'Have you seen the great Eagle who stole my red velvet slippers?' Each stanza ends with, 'And Nella wept.' The flight of the birds overhead is almost dreamlike.

Be sure to end the story as it began with Nella dancing 'under thousands of stars, amongst thousands of coloured lights,' while the people shout 'Brava, Nella! Brava, brava!'

A gay, inconsequential yet satisfying story, especially suitable for girls, so many of whom dream of becoming dancers.

The Farmer's Wife and the Tiger

Telling time: 8 minutes.
Audience: Boys and girls of 8–10.

A story from Pakistan typical of its country of origin. It is published in a collection prepared by the Asian Cultural Centre for Unesco in Tokyo. It has a national flavour in its details—the use of oxen for ploughing, the native dress of the characters, the tiger and the jackal as part of everyday life. The theme is typical of folklore everywhere, the bully defeated by native cunning rather than physical strength.

There are four characters to be portrayed here. First of all the tiger who is a coward in spite of his strength. The farmer too is a coward and leans heavily on his wife's resourcefulness. The wife has commonsense, a quick brain, courage and bravado. The jackal, a typical sychophant, is dependent on the tiger's leavings but despises him nevertheless.

So the stage is set for a story with drama, suspense and considerable humour. The encounter between the farmer and the tiger is by way of introduction, with its polite phrases which neither party means, and the revelation that the tiger means to eat the farmer's oxen. With the entrance of the woman, the pace quickens and her abuse of her husband is spoken with relish. Directly she takes over, there is action—she rides away dressed as a man, her bold threats against the tiger terrify him, her quick repartee when the tiger and his jackal return, clinches the defeat. Be sure the children don't miss the fun of the tiger and the jackal tying their tails together with a reef-knot. This is a story to laugh at in spite of the fate of the two animals which, after all, is deserved.

Everest Climbed

Telling time: 10 minutes.
Audience: Children of 10 upwards, particularly boys.

Ian Serraillier is a master of the story in verse. He has written many poems of this kind, some in ballad form as the Robin Hood stories, others from fairy tales or legends. Some readers will know his poem about the voyage of the Kon-tiki. On this occasion I have chosen to include the story of a great adventure which took place at the time of the Coronation of our Queen, Elizabeth the Second.

The climbing of mountains has inspired many poets. Here we have the ascent of the highest of them all, Mount Everest, so long a challenge to mountaineers. I have chosen the final section of the poem, the assault on the summit by Edmund Hillary and Tensing. The account is quite factual, as anyone who has read Hillary's own story will recognize. Yet it is a poet's view. This inclusion of prosaic detail in a poem can be a good introduction for children who regard poetry as divorced from everyday life.

We follow the climb, step by step, in all its hardship and the physical misery of such adventures. The summit seems out of reach and unobtainable:

> 'All day the windy peak flared
> In foam-white flame . . .'

The summit ridge is terrifying:

> 'On one side darkly the mountain dropped,
> On the other two plunging miles of peak
> Shot from the dizzy skyline down
> In a silver streak.'

Only after great peril do the two exhausted men set foot on the summit.

Poetry only comes into its own when it is spoken and it must be spoken well. It needs to be absorbed, learned word perfect and said aloud many times before being presented to an audience. Follow the punctuation implicitly, for this is how the author meant it to be read and this alone brings out what he wanted to say.

It does no harm in these days of debunking of great men and heroic deeds, to remind young people of a brave adventure, a challenge to elemental forces, with all the odds against success.

Poor Old Lady, She Swallowed a Fly

Audience: Boys and girls of about 10.

This ridiculous 'poem' has become a favourite with children. The storyteller will be the narrator but the children can supply the chorus, that is, the two recurring lines, 'I don't know why she swallowed a fly,/ Poor old lady, I think she'll die.'

It helps with audience participation if the narrator adds the appropriate sound as each insect or animal is introduced. So 'She swallowed a cat' would call forth 'Mee-ow', a dog 'Bow-wow' and so on. The children soon catch this up and join in. What noise does a spider make? I don't know, so I substitute 'Ugh!' which is most people's rather unfair reaction to a spider.

So the last verse would become (with the children's help):

> 'She swallowed a cow . . . *Mooo-ooo!*
> She swallowed the cow to catch the dog, *Bow-wow!*
> She swallowed the dog to catch the cat, *Mee-ow!*
> She swallowed the cat to catch the bird, *Tweet-tweet!*
> She swallowed the bird to catch the spider, *Ugh!*
> She swallowed the spider to catch the fly, *Buzz-buzz!*

The final two lines will need practice to ensure the right effect of surprise.

This rhyme, like *I went to the Animal Fair*, is for that sometimes necessary hiatus between stories when children are becoming restive.

Room for a Little One

Telling time: 6 minutes.
Audience: 8 upwards and adults.
Occasion: Christmas.

A moving Christmas story which could well be told to any group of children whether in a church, a Sunday School, a library or a school. It is a kind of folk tale and was told by a farmer's wife in Somerset seventy-five years ago. It is an example of oral tradition but surely bears the stamp of a storyteller's personality.

The form of this story raises the problem of dialect in storytelling. How much should one use it? Surely not so strongly that it puzzles the audience and causes children to lose the sense of the story. It is quite possible to *suggest* a dialect by the introduction of a few local words and a turn of phrase. Here the dialect used is that of Somerset, but the story could be told in any dialect in which the storyteller is at home. The only unfamiliar word is 'nirrip' and this can be either explained beforehand or replaced by 'donkey'.

The keynote of the story is tenderness and compassion. It will be obvious to most children that this is a version of the Bible Christmas story but set in England in our own time. This should add to its appeal and help to bring its meaning home to children.

It needs to be told as a straightforward narrative with no dramatic trimmings or attempts to personify the little 'nirrip' and the old ox. There is a vivid feeling of the bitter cold of the countryside and the suffering of the serving maid and her humble companions—'their feet they was blue-ice blocks'. The bitter weariness of the old ox, unwanted by everyone because of his age, has significance too. But this is not a sentimental story for Bridget and her companions are not sorry for themselves, their hearts are too full of compassion for others.

Even the unfortunate of the world have their moments of joy and the climax of the story brings one of these to Bridget and her friends so that there is almost a feeling of ecstasy. On this note of joy and triumph the story should end. Lit by the star the poor stable is a place of glory. 'God's dear Son' is there and the air is full of heavenly music in which even the little 'nirrip' joins, forgetting for once his hoarse unmusical voice. If we can convey this feeling, we have given the children a memorable experience.

This is a story which must be part of the storyteller, so that he can give himself to it with sincerity and with no thought of himself.

The Hero

Telling time: 4–5 minutes.
Audience: Children of 8 upwards and adults.

Nearly all the stories in this book are for telling to children, but here is one that is for telling to adults by a child. It was written by the Indian poet, Rabindranath Tagore, but it has the authentic voice of a child. Would not most small boys like to be the hero of an imaginary adventure like this? How satisfactory to be able to protect helpless adults instead of being protected by them. Truly it would be like 'a story in a book'!

This is a story that can easily be learnt by heart. Indeed it must be told in the same words for it is a translation of a poem, hence its form. For storytelling it should be told as a continuous narrative. It begins quietly as the scene is set and gains pace and excitement as the boy's imagination catches fire. Enjoy it as the boy does and linger over such phrases as 'Mother, just you watch me!' The boy enjoys the gory nature of the fight, 'A great number of the robbers are cut to pieces!' he says with satisfaction, and, 'I come to you all stained with blood!'

How delightful to be praised by your family and the servants. Here, when I am telling the story, I alter the order a little. It would seem natural to keep all the praise together, so I put the last two sentences of the story to follow after his mother's, 'I don't know what I should do if I hadn't my boy to escort me.' This allows the new final sentence to correspond with the boy's change of mood. Reality has struck and the adventure is recognized for what it is, a delightful dream. Your voice will show the boy's disillusion, 'A thousand useless things happen day after day, and why couldn't such a thing come true by chance?' Then repeat slowly and longingly, 'It would be like a story in a book.'

I have told this short story to both children and adults. It is particularly appreciated by parents—perhaps they hear the echo of their own sons in it.

High Flight

Audience: Slightly older children.

This poem was written by a young Canadian Pilot Officer who was killed in the Battle of Britain at the age of nineteen. His early death adds poignancy to the poet's ecstasy in his flight through 'footless halls of air' and his sense of the presence of God. A poem like this could well follow a story of not necessarily successful achievement, but of high endeavour. It not only describes an experience dreamed of by many boys, but, given the right moment, it strikes a note to which boys will respond.

The Merry-go-round

Telling time: 20 minutes.
Audience: Boys and girls of 8 upwards.

Alison Uttley has a gift for writing tales of magic and enchantment; stories which excite wonder and yet are set in an everyday environment. She says herself (quoted in a welcome reprint of some of her tales, chosen by Kathleen Lines, *Fairy Tales by Alison Uttley*, published by Faber and Faber): 'So each and every tale holds everyday magic, and each is connected with awareness of everyday life, when reality is made visible, and one sees what goes on with new eyes.'

This particular story comes from a collection called *John Barleycorn*, first published in 1948. The merry-go-round is, alas, seldom seen nowadays. In my own childhood it was a familiar and exciting annual visitor to country districts. It was driven by steam and the mounts were always gaily painted wooden horses. It is these merry-go-round horses that are the central figures in this story.

Try to make the two country boys, Michael and John, individuals, for they *are* different. They accept their magical experience as real at the time. It is only afterwards that they wonder if it was all a dream.

The story is in three parts: the introduction to the Fair and Mrs Lee's gift of the Roman whistle; the night adventure with the merry-go-round horses; the postscript with the open ending that suggests the whistle might be blown again. What would happen then? Ah, who knows!

A variation in pace is important. At first when the boys awake in the moonlit night with its evocative sounds and scents, the story moves quietly, but when they mount the little horses, the pace increases with the growing excitement. As the boys ride Hot Fun and Spit Fire, they have a feeling of bliss, for an experience like this is the realization of a dream. When the ride is over and the horses climb on to their wooden stands again, the pace of the storytelling quietens down too.

If time dictates a shortening of this rather long story, it can be carried out most easily in the descriptive and nostalgic passages. It would be helpful first, though, to talk with the children before telling the story, to find out what they know about fairs.

This is a lively story and even the dream-like episode is full of movement and action. Enjoy it with the children—it is usually a favourite.

The Hare and the Baboons

Telling time: 5 minutes.
Audience: Children of 6 upwards.

This is a story from Africa which always amuses children. It is in the Brer Rabbit tradition, for these stories gathered orally from Central Africa often have their counterpart in Joel Chandler Harris's collections gathered in North America. This is the kind of story which would be told round a camp fire at the end of the day. In Africa it is the Hare—the Little Wise One—who lives in the moon, not a man.

Hare is small and cannot climb; the Baboons are large and can climb, so they play this unkind trick on Hare. Hare has brains, the Baboons are stupid, so Hare is able to trick them in an ingenious way. Baboons, by the way, walk on their hands, hence the aptness of Hare's plan.

Children soon realize what will happen and can be seen looking at their own (probably grimy) hands surreptitiously. Although the Baboons are punished rightly, there is often a sneaking feeling of pity for them. After all, who wants to wash his hands all that number of times—or even once!

In the first part of the story, Hare must seem a little pathetic, later he is smug and self-righteous. One can imagine him thinking, 'Clever me!' The formality of the conversation between Hare and the Baboons must be maintained and a slight variation of the voice will indicate whether the Hare or the Baboons are speaking.

A story which can be used at any time, especially when there are African children present, for this is part of their own tradition.

I went to the Animal Fair

Audience: Boys and girls of 8–10.

It is helpful to have the words of this rhyme written on a large sheet of paper which can be displayed. A nonsense-participation rhyme like this is useful between stories when children begin to grow tired of listening.

Many children will know the simple tune to which this is usually sung, but music is not essential. Children will be familiar with the words too, so that they are reasonably fluent. Keep it going rhythmically, hoping that everyone will finish together on the words 'monkey, monkey, monk' and be ready to start again immediately. Quicken the pace on the second repetition, beating time if necessary. By the third time round, the children will be bubbling over with laughter as they vie with each other to keep up the faster pace and to be the last to fall out. A few simple but optional movements help in the fun—'combing his auburn hair', 'gave a jump', 'the elephant sneezed' . . .

No literary claims are made for this rhyme—it's just fun!

The Signalman

Telling time: 12 minutes.
Audience: Older boys and girls and adults.
Occasion: As an introduction to Dickens.

A most effective story which has a really eerie atmosphere. Let the audience enjoy it and agree that it is a good story before telling them that it is by Dickens, an author whom many young people consider dull and old-fashioned.

I have kept the author's words throughout but I have abridged the story for telling. A few words of introduction about the narrator of the story will help to introduce it—this is not a story of the railway today. The atmosphere is strange from the beginning and it becomes more and more menacing as the narrator descends into the deep cutting with its clammy stone, gloomy red light and its 'earthy, deadly smell'. As we hear of the supernatural being the signalman has seen, with 'the left arm across the face and the right arm gesticulating with the utmost passion', we see it too and feel a cold shudder run down our spines. The signalman is a haunted man—he must tell his story with dread and with glances over his shoulder.

After the description of the accident, I omit a second accident which seemed to me to lessen the impact of the first and to make too long an interval before the climax of the story, the signalman's own death. This is a dramatic surprise, yet from the moment when the narrator sees the men gathered below in the cutting, he knows—and we know—that the disaster the signalman feared has happened.

The natural ending for the story is the single sentence, 'It was the signalman's own death that the spectre had foretold.' In the original there is another brief paragraph which seems superfluous.

The story is rich in telling phrases, pure Dickensian, which help to create the atmosphere, 'A vague vibration in the earth and air, quickly changing into a violent pulsation and an oncoming rush . . . The wind and the wires took up the story with a long lamenting wail . . .' It is essential to keep the identical phrase used by both the narrator and the spectre, 'Halloa! Below there!' for it is this which has such terrible significance for the signalman. The gestures of the spectre could well be used so that the audience can visualize them, 'the left arm over the face and the right arm violently waved'. That the face of the ghost is never seen intensifies the horror of the visitation and that the signalman is the only one to see the apparition adds to his despair.

It is well worth spending time on the preparation of this story as an antidote to the many trivial ghost tales found in anthologies today.

Two of Everything

Telling time: 10 minutes.
Audience: Children of 8 upwards.

An amusing folk tale with a natural homespun sense of fun. It begins quite factually with a very poor and hardworking couple. So poor is Mrs Hak-Tak—a name which sounds comic to children—that she has only one hairpin. Then comes the surprise, for Mr Hak-Tak finds a big brass pot in his vegetable plot.

This is the introduction. Mr and Mrs Hak-Tak are not clever people and they discover only gradually the powers of the magic pot—to make two of everything that is dropped into it. This makes the story a good one for the slower child for he, too, can go at his own pace until he reaches the proud moment when he guesses what will happen *before* Mr and Mrs Hak-Tak do.

To help the child to anticipate, pause before the climax of the story when Mrs Hak-Tak falls into the pot herself. When Mr Hak-Tak does the same thing, I have heard a child cry a warning spontaneously, 'Look out!' for he has guessed what must happen. That the two old people should fall into the brass pot seems comic to children with their unsophisticated sense of humour.

The old couple should not be portrayed as stupid or greedy; they are neither, in fact they are rather endearing in their simplicity.

A good-natured amusing story, *Two of Everything* is an exercise in anticipation for the audience. It has the homely wisdom and wry humour of the true folk tale.

The Good Little Christmas Tree

Telling time: 15 minutes.
Audience: Children of 6 upwards.
Occasion: Christmas.

This is a great favourite with children because of its cumlative repetition and its Christmassy feeling. It is indeed a perfect story to tell at Christmas for it has all the essentials, family affection, compassion, the joy of giving and the anticipation of receiving. It is set against a snowy landscape and the central figure is a Christmas tree. It is typical of its author in its imagination and warmth of feeling.

The little Christmas Tree is looking for trimmings for his branches and he pays for them with his own needles and, sometimes, with a bite from the cookies the children's mother has hung on his branches. Each acquisition adds a phrase to the rhythmic chant—'the diamonds glittering, toadstools gleaming . . .' Each time the chant ends with the same sentence, 'The cookies bobbing about like little brown mice.' These phrases must be memorized and well practised and must always remain the same, so that the children can join in if they wish. To visualize the items helps the storyteller to remember them. In the final repetition at the end of the story the author has increased the impact by using stronger adjectives—the diamonds flash not glitter, the candles flame not flicker. This can be appreciated when one is reading to oneself, but for telling it is necessary to keep the same phrases throughout or the children will be confused and unable to participate.

The characters whom the Christmas Tree meets can be suggested with what ingenuity the storyteller wishes. The wolves growl, the goblins mutter crossly, and so on, but the story will be just as effective without these aids to imagination.

There is a change of mood when the little Christmas Tree sees his reflection in a pool and realizes that he no longer has his fresh green needles and a pleasing shape. His unhappiness is very real to children and they feel sympathy, and this emotion makes the way in which Father Christmas brings happiness again all the more enjoyable. 'We will go home together,' he says. The procession of all the characters in the story forms, the pace quickens until everyone is chanting the familiar phrases, ending triumphantly with, 'And the cookies bobbing about like little brown mice.'

And here I would end. No more is needed. The story has come full circle.